African & Caribbean Folktales, Myths & Legends

For Lauren and Scarlett.

African & Caribbean Folktales, Myths & Legends

by **Wendy Shearer**

Illustrated by Andrea Pippins

SCHOLASTIC

Published in the UK by Scholastic, 2021
Euston House, 24 Eversholt Street, London, NW1 1DB
Scholastic Ireland, 89E Lagan Road, Dublin Industrial Estate,
Glasnevin, Dublin, D11 HP5F

ISBN 978-93-5471-818-2

A CIP catalogue record for this book is available from the British Library.

www.scholastic.co.uk

This reprint edition September 2024

Printed in India at Shivam Offset Press, New Delhi

Contents

Spirits And Shape-Shifters

Myths and Legends

Legends

Introduction

"A story, a story, let it come, let it go!" —West African saying

Storytelling has been part of African and Caribbean culture for hundreds of years. The stories in this collection are a selection of folktales, myths and legends from both regions. Many were not written down until the early nineteenth century by collectors but had been told for hundreds of years before that.

In Africa, stories are traditionally passed down orally, usually by a travelling musician and historian called a griot, the keeper of their area's history and traditions. In the Caribbean islands, stories are told and retold in the evenings, when friends and families are gathered together outside under the stars. Most of the Caribbean stories originated in Africa, carried to the islands by enslaved Africans. The stories were then influenced by European and East Indian folklore. In this way, the wonderful stories in this book have travelled and changed with each telling and each storyteller.

Jack Mandora, me nuh choose none. —Jamaican saying

Jack Mandora (keeper of stories), *I have told the story the way I heard it.*

Folktales

Folktales are ancient stories which were passed down by word of mouth to keep traditions alive and guide people in all parts of their lives. They are stories filled with animals and spirits who can talk and behave like humans. This delightful collection of folktales has been grouped into popular themes of Tricksters, Magic and Mystery, and Spirits and Shape-shifters. They are all filled with characters unique to the island countries and different regions across Africa.

Trickster Tales

In these stories you will find people and animals who use their clever wits to get what they want – but beware! Sometimes even the trickster gets tricked.

The Headless Dance

This is a popular folktale from Cuba, an island in the Caribbean. It is known as an origin tale that explains what happened at the beginning of the world. It features Cuban music, dancing and devils . . .

In the beginning, when the world was still forming beautiful mountains, forests and seas, the devil and his family lived right here on earth. There was El Diablo, the devil himself, his wife, La Diabla, and their little devil son, El Diablito. They lived side by side with the animals who roamed freely in the neighbourhood. Everyone lived in harmony with each other . . . most of the time.

The only problem was that the devil and his family weren't the best people to have living as your neighbours – not because they were mean or unkind or anything like that.

It's just that the devil and his family were extremely loud. Everything they did was loud! El Diablo loved to dance and could rumba and tango for hours, late into the evening. His son, El Diablito, loved to play the quinto, a type of conga drum, banging out rhythms while his papa danced. La Diabla loved to sing while she cooked. Her voice would rise to the treetops and – if you weren't too distracted by all the noise – you could smell her delicious empanadas and tamales whenever you walked past their kitchen.

So, on any given night, the neighbourhood was thumping with the devils' music and loud voices, and shaking with their wild dance moves. And it wasn't just their enthusiasm for partying that was loud. They also had a habit of setting their house on fire! Every time El Diablo and his wife had a fierce row, one of them would storm out and slam the wooden doors, which would then burst into flames. That's how it is when you have parents who are devils. Poor little El Diablito never knew if he would have a bed to sleep in or a pile of ashes.

The turkeys, *los guanajos*, lived in a barn directly behind the devils' house. They often had the job of flapping their turkey wings to put out the flames, or screeching for help to collect water from the river to stop any fires from spreading.

One evening the devils were cooking up a feast in their kitchen. El Diablo blew some flames through his nostrils, to make his food extra crispy. He did not notice when the flames leaped up from his food and on to the window. He strolled into the next room, leaving the kitchen to go up in flames. One of the turkeys, who just happened to be in his garden next door, saw the fire through the window. The flames were rising high and starting to spread along the ground towards their barn. He quickly called out to his turkey friends for help. It took several hours, lots of turkey flapping and the strength of a mighty buffalo to finally put the fire out.

"That is the last time I will put out one of their fires!" screeched one of the turkeys. They were fed up with the devils and decided that something must be done about them. So the next morning after the terrible blaze, a few animals gathered secretly in a cave hidden behind a waterfall to discuss the devils' antics.

Mongoose spoke up first. "We need to do something about those devils, otherwise the rivers will run dry and the forest will burn down."

White Bull flared his nostrils and nodded in agreement.

"I couldn't get to sleep last night," complained one of the turkeys. "After we put out the fire, El Diablo was jumping up so high, I could see his head bouncing above his roof. Up and down, up and down, for hours." She tucked her turkey head under her wing and popped it up again to demonstrate. That's when the eldest turkey had an idea.

"That's how we can get rid of them. We hold a headless dance!"

"A headless dance?" asked the other turkey, confused.

"What do you mean?" Iguana wondered. "A dance without our heads?"

"Yes. Well, almost." The eldest turkey explained: "Just now, when you tucked your head under your wing, you looked like your head had been cut off. If we all tuck our heads under our wings and pretend we have no heads, we can say we're having a headless dance."

"How will that help?" White Bull huffed and puffed impatiently.

"We'll tell the devils they can only join in our dance if they let us cut off their heads first." He giggled at the thought of all the animals tucking their heads down, pretending to be headless on the dance floor.

"They'll never fall for it," Mongoose said flatly.

Iguana, who was hanging upside down on the cave wall, asked, "Why would they even want to join in?"

"Because they cannot resist dancing," said the turkey. "They'll hear the music and see all of us turkeys dancing without our heads.

"*Bailar sin cabeza!* The headless dance!" all the animals shouted, agreeing it was a very good idea.

The dance was held the very next evening, just as the sun dipped behind the trees. Twelve turkeys tucked their heads under their wings and began dancing wildly to the sound of the band. The monkeys, or *bongoceros*, were playing the drums, and the golden-headed finches sang their hearts out to the rhythms.

Back at the home of the devils, a row was simmering in the kitchen between El Diablo and La Diabla over who could make the tastiest mojo sauce.

"Everyone knows mine is the best," fumed La Diabla.

"You always add too much sour orange juice," snapped El Diablo.

"I'm going to get some peace and quiet," said El Diablito, leaving the house. He was fed up with seeing his parents fight night after night and wanted to find a quiet spot to read until they had both stopped arguing.

"El Diablito told me he prefers *my* mojo sauce." La Diabla smiled at her husband triumphantly and tapped her long claws on the table. El Diablo's face turned beetroot red. He was so outraged that he stormed out of the house. His long legs leaped over the valley as he made his way towards the mountains. He stomped along, raging to himself about his wife. "My sauce is far better than hers. What does she know anyway?"

Despite his anger, and how far he'd walked – all the way to the highest mountaintop – he felt the familiar beats of bongo drums and heard the shrill sound of birds singing in the distance. He followed the irresistible rhythm until he arrived at a hall where White Bull and Iguana were guarding the door. *This must be an excellent party if these two are needed to guard the door*, thought El Diablo. He imagined a long hall covered in strings of bright lights and colourful decorations, with everyone dancing in the middle. He could not wait to join in.

"Good evening, my friends. It sounds like a fabulous party. I'm ready to dance." El Diablo spun around on his heels and then tried to enter. White Bull stepped in front of the door, blocking El Diablo's way.

"No, no, no. You have to remove your head first. This is a headless dance," said White Bull.

"A headless dance?" asked El Diablo. He wondered if he had heard correctly.

"That's right. Anyone who wants to come in, must have their heads cut off." White Bull stared straight at the devil and did not crack a smile.

El Diablo thought it must be a joke, but White Bull and Iguana looked very serious. "Let me see first," said the devil. He was curious and tried to peer inside through the door. He could not believe what he was seeing! There were headless turkeys dancing dramatically with each other, monkeys banging the bongos and shaking the chekeré, tree frogs ringing their cowbells. There was not a single head in sight! And so he believed that they must have all been cut off. Even the birds were singing:

> *Baile sin cabeza! Si no tienes cabeza, puedes bailar!*
> Headless dance! If you have no head, you can dance!

El Diablo loved to dance and really wanted to go inside, but he was not sure about losing his head.

Iguana was starting to worry that El Diablo would not agree, so he said, "I'm sorry, El Diablo, but these are the rules. No one else minds."

"You don't need your head for dancing anyway." White Bull shrugged and sounded as though it was not a big deal to cut off your head. Inside the hall, the animals wondered what was taking so long. They played their instruments louder and the birds sang even more sweetly. El Diablo's feet started tapping and his knees started bending in time to the band. His body was moving in the direction of the door. Iguana closed his eyes and held his breath. What if their plan did not work? The devil could set them all on fire!

"You are right, White Bull. I don't need my head for dancing. My legs do all the fancy moves. Take off my head so I can join in," El Diablo agreed finally.

Iguana opened his eyes and did not hesitate for a second. He quickly chopped off the devil's head. He put his hands to his mouth and let out a long whistle. Black Crow had been listening from the trees and knew this was a sign for her to collect a devil's head. She flew down from the trees, picked up the head and carried it away.

"One devil down, two more to go!" said White Bull to the turkeys. They lifted up their heads from beneath their wings to see if it was true. Yes, their plan was working!

"One devil down, one devil down!" The turkeys cheered with happiness.

Meanwhile, La Diabla was waiting for her husband to come home. She silently raged, thinking he was deliberately staying out late to annoy her. When her patience finally wore thin, she went to find him. The whole house burst into ruby-red flames as she slammed the door behind her.

It was not long before she, too, heard the *bongoceros* playing their bongos in the distance.

"I bet he has gone dancing," she seethed, and off she stomped over the valley towards the sound of the music. She was so angry that her tail dragged along the ground, creating smoke and sparking little fires. Coming to the barn door, La Diabla tried to push past White Bull and Iguana, but they held firm and refused her entry.

"You have to remove your head first. This is a headless dance," said White Bull.

"A headless dance?" she asked, looking very puzzled. "Is my husband inside?"

Iguana shrugged. "Maybe. We don't know. Why don't you look?"

She was curious and tried to peer through the door. Just as El Diablo had, she saw headless turkeys dancing dramatically with each other, monkeys banging the bongos and shaking the chekeré, tree frogs ringing their cowbells and birds singing:

> *Baile sin cabeza! Si no tienes cabeza, puedes bailar!*
> Headless dance! If you have no head, you can dance!

"How are they dancing without their heads?" La Diabla asked, and threw up her arms in disbelief.

"It's easy. Anyone can do it," replied Iguana.

"Well, why have you still got *your* heads?" she asked suspiciously.

"Because we're not dancing," said White Bull, and kept his face serious.

La Diabla narrowed her eyes and shot them a fiery look. Iguana gulped nervously. He did not think she believed them. La Diabla could not see if her husband was inside, so she said, "Well, if this is the only way for me to go in and check . . ."

Iguana moved towards her, ready to cut off her head, but she suddenly twisted her neck round and glared at him.

"I have my eyes on you, Iguana. Be careful with my head."

Iguana gulped, and swiftly chopped off her head. He put his hands to his mouth and let out a long whistle. Black Crow flew down from the tree and carried the head away.

"Two devils down, one more to go!" said White Bull to the turkeys, and they all cheered with delight.

El Diablito returned to a pile of ashes where

his house used to be. He was extremely worried because his parents often started fires but had never completely burned down the house before. He decided to go and look for them. He had walked over the valley and headed towards the mountains when he heard the sound of music. Knowing that his parents both loved to dance, he followed the sounds to the dance hall where White Bull and Iguana stood outside guarding the door.

"Are my parents inside?" El Diablito asked.

Iguana shrugged. "Maybe. We don't know."

"Can I go inside to look for them?" he said.

"You have to remove your head first. This is a headless dance," said White Bull.

El Diablito tried to peer inside through the door. He saw headless turkeys dancing dramatically with each other, monkeys banging the bongos and shaking the chekeré, tree frogs ringing their cowbells and birds singing:

> *Baile sin cabeza! Si no tienes cabeza, puedes bailar!*
> Headless dance! If you have no head, you can dance!

He turned to White Bull and Iguana and said, "I don't want to stay and dance. I only want to know if my parents are here."

White Bull and Iguana shook their heads and refused to let him in. "This is *el baile sin cabeza* – the headless dance. You cannot go in unless we remove your head."

El Diablito was tempted for a moment. He thought to himself that it might be nice to go inside and hang out with the band playing their instruments. After all, he loved banging noisily on his conga drum too. And the turkeys did look like they were having a great time dancing without their heads.

"Please open the door so I can look in from right here," El Diablito said politely.

Iguana looked at White Bull. White Bull looked at Iguana. They did not know what to say. The turkeys stopped dancing. The monkeys stopped playing. Everyone listened closely for their reply.

"No. We cannot." White Bull puffed up his chest and squared off his shoulders.

"Rules are rules," said Iguana.

The monkeys nervously started to play once more. The turkeys peeped through their wings and carried on dancing. Now the birds were singing even louder:

> *Baile sin cabeza! Baile sin cabeza!*
> Headless dance! Headless dance!

Black Crow flew down too early, thinking that the last devil's head was ready. He dug his feet into El Diablito's curly hair and tried to fly off with his head.

"Not yet!" cried out Iguana, and shooed Black Crow away. El Diablito was on his guard. He knew that the animals were up to something. His sharp eyes saw how nervous Iguana looked. He sniffed the air with his long, pointy nose. *I smell a trap*, he thought to himself, and suddenly made up his mind not to go inside. Unlike his parents, he was far too clever to be tricked by the animals' story.

"I'm not really much of a dancer anyway and it is getting late," he said to White Bull and Iguana. "I think I will go back home." He walked away from the dance hall and hid nearby in the forest. He watched and waited for the animals to come out.

"We've lost the last devil," White Bull announced to the turkeys and suddenly the music and dancing stopped. The eldest turkey came out flapping with his head firmly fixed on his body.

"How could you let the last devil go without removing his head?" he shrieked loud enough for El Diablito to hear. His little devil ears pricked up and he listened in.

"They tricked my parents!" he said to himself bitterly. His green eyes flashed and smoke hissed from his nose. He felt angry about what had happened to his parents and shocked at how close he had come to losing his own head. *Well, I can play my own tricks too*, he thought, planning to get his revenge. He tunnelled a hole deep down in the earth and sat plotting. Ideas of how to trick the animals came to him, making him chuckle with delight as he pictured their faces. The next evening, when all the animals in the neighbourhood were settling down for the night, El Diablito began playing his tricks. He flashed through their homes, slamming doors and smashing plates, moving objects or terrifying them with an unsuspecting noise.

The animals never knew when El Diablito was near, but they saw signs of his presence when things were set on fire or disappeared. He became known as the quiet little devil, lurking in trees and hiding in shadows. His laughter could be heard echoing into the night, after leaving a burning footprint or giving someone a fright. No one has ever been able to catch him in the act. Which is why people say that the devil is still around, right here, in our world today.

Monkey Liver Soup

(Trinidad and Tobago)

This is a popular folktale from the Caribbean islands. There are versions told in Trinidad, Grenada and Jamaica, and this particular version is inspired by Guyanese storyteller, Ken Corsbie. It is the story of how Crocodile tries to steal Monkey's liver and ends up getting tricked himself. A variation of this story is also told along the Swahili coast of south-east Africa, where Shark tries to steal Monkey's heart.

There once was a crocodile who lived in a dark, muddy swamp along the Nariva River. He was feeling extremely worried because his wife was sick and he didn't know how to help her. He called Doctor Python, who had a very good reputation for diagnosing rare illnesses.

"Crocky, my friend, you've got a difficult time ahead of you," said the snake doctor, unravelling his stethoscope from his long snaky body.

"What is it? Is it serious?" asked Crocodile, wondering if he should be worried about his wife.

"It is serious, and I'm afraid there's not much that you can do. There is a cure, but it is very difficult to find," the doctor replied.

"Tell me, Doc. Whatever it is, I will find it for my wife," said Crocodile.

The doctor explained that Crocodile's wife would only get better if she drank some monkey liver soup.

"WHAT?" yelled Crocodile, horrified at the thought. "Monkey liver soup? How will I make monkey liver soup?" Crocodile knew that monkeys spent most of their time out of his reach, swinging from tree to tree. He had never before managed to catch one.

"Exactly! That's why no one ever gets better from

this sickness," said the doctor, shaking his head sadly. "You need to get hold of a monkey's liver and cook it with some sweet potato, yam and green banana to make a nice pot of heart-warming soup," he recommended. Crocodile watched his wife sadly as the doctor slithered away. *At least there is some hope*, he thought. *I'll just have to come up with a plan.* So he settled down in the swamp and began to think hard.

The next day, Crocodile left his murky swamp in search of a monkey. He made his way slowly, gliding along the river. He looked closely at the trees along the riverbank, hoping to see a monkey swinging by when, *SPLASH*, he bumped into Manatee, the large sea cow.

"Oops, sorry, Crocky. I didn't see you there. What are you doing out of your swamp?" asked Manatee.

"Oh, I'm just taking a swim. Looking to see if anyone new is about," said Crocodile slyly. He did not want to trust Manatee with his plan, just in case he warned the monkeys.

"I heard that everyone hangs out by Manzilla Bay these days. That's where the best fruit is," said Manatee, taking a big gulp of air before he swam back down to the bottom of the river.

That sounded like a good place to look for monkeys, thought Crocodile, and so he headed out into the wide river.

It wasn't long before he reached the bank by Manzilla Bay. He sank into the water, lowering his long tail and keeping only his beady eyes just above the water, not wanting to be seen. But after a few moments of quiet waiting, he suddenly felt something pelt him on the head.

"OUCH." Before he could open his eyes, he felt something hard land on his tail. "OWWW."

He looked up and saw Monkey hanging from a balata tree.

"Watch where you're throwing those shells, Monkey!" yelled Crocodile.

"Ah, sorry, Crocky," giggled Monkey. "I didn't see you there. You sneaked up so quietly."

"Hm. I'm just gliding along." Crocodile smiled slyly to himself. The first part of his plan was working – he'd found a monkey. Now to trick him out of his liver! He tried to sound casual so that Monkey would not suspect anything.

"What brings you upstream, Crocky?" asked Monkey as he removed the pips from his balata fruit. Crocodile nearly blurted out his plan to catch Monkey, but managed to think of an excuse quickly. "Er, I'm just taking a break from the party down by the lagoon."

Monkey sat straight up and stopped peeling his fruit. He could never resist a party.

"There's a party down by the lagoon?" he asked. "What fun! How come I didn't hear about it?"

"Eh, eh, I'm surprised you didn't know. Everyone's there. You should come." Crocodile smiled, revealing his sparkling, sharp teeth.

"Come on, Crocky man, you know I can't swim. How would I get across to the lagoon?" huffed Monkey.

Crocodile swam right up to the bank and swung his long tail under the balata tree. "You don't have to worry about swimming. I am a great swimmer. You can ride on my back," he offered, with the most sincere smile he could muster.

Monkey thought about it for a moment.

"Is there music?" he asked.

"Oh yes," said Crocodile. "The toucans are playing their steel pan drums."

"What about fruit trees? Are there plenty of fruit trees?"

"Of course, Monkey, man! That's why the party

is there. Lots of the sweetest fruit trees grow around that lagoon."

Monkey hesitated. Crocodile had a habit of biting anyone he wanted when he was cross. It was best not to get close to his sharp teeth. He wasn't sure if he could trust Crocodile; he might turn around and go *SNAP* at any moment. "I don't know, Crocky. Monkeys and water don't mix. If I fall in the water, I will surely drown. I think I'll just stay up here in my tree."

"Suit yourself. I thought you liked parties. But the offer for a ride is there." Crocodile turned around slowly to head back into the water.

"Hold on, hold on. Wait up!" Monkey jumped down from the tree and stood at the edge of the riverbank. He stroked his white beard and thought for a moment. "If I sit on your back, you must promise to move really slowly."

"Yes, really slowly."

"No bumping around."

"Of course, no bumping around."

"And no swishing your tail either."

"OK. No swishing my tail."

"Because I might fall off if you swish your tail."

"Don't worry, I'll be steady. Just climb on to my

back, Monkey." Crocodile sank his long teeth just beneath the water to hide his smile. He was so pleased at how his plan was unfolding.

Monkey stopped suddenly, suspiciously looking at Crocodile. "Why are you so keen for me to go to this party, Crocky?"

"Hey, it doesn't bother me if you go or not. It's easy for me to swim there and it seems a shame for you to miss out on all those juicy sweet balatas and giant pomerac fruits." Crocodile smiled his toothy grin, trying not to look too eager.

Monkey's ears pricked up at the mention of giant pomeracs. He imagined the pear-shaped fruit, hanging like crimson jewels waiting to be snatched and eaten. He was getting a bit tired of only eating tiny balatas. It took such a long time to peel off the skin and he needed to eat so many to fill himself up.

"All right, you've convinced me. I'll come with you," said Monkey. Crocodile moved closer to the bank and Monkey stepped gingerly on to his long mouth and walked towards the middle of his back. He sat very carefully on his rough scales and tried to make himself comfortable. He looked nervously at the muddy water as Crocodile glided away from the riverbank. They made their way downstream, twisting and turning as the river snaked along towards the lagoon. Monkey sat very still while they drifted past the red mangroves. He was so worried about falling into the water that he didn't even try to grab any juicy red pomerac fruit from the overhanging trees. Crocodile was silent for a long time, with only the slits of his eyes and his nostrils above the water. They were right in the middle of the river now and Monkey began to feel nervous. He really was not comfortable being so close to the water and they were too far from either side of the riverbanks for him to jump off and scamper back into the trees.

"Hey, Crocky! CROCKY! Are you awake?" *THUD THUD THUD*. He tapped Crocodile on the head with his hand. "Don't fall asleep, man. This is a serious business. I can't fall into this river. Remember I can't swim." Monkey was on his feet now, his face twitching from left to right, eyeing up the water either side of him.

Crocodile lifted his long jaws out of the water and gritted his teeth. He wanted to turn around and go *SNAP* on to Monkey's leg, but he had to get closer to home first, to be sure he wouldn't lose Monkey and his precious liver in the water. "Of course I'm awake, Monkey. Just sit down and enjoy the ride." Crocodile lowered his face into the water, keeping his jaws firmly shut so that he would not be tempted to bite Monkey.

They came to a fork in the river where one way led to the swamp and the other way led to the lagoon. Crocodile took the left fork towards the swamp and Monkey noticed immediately.

"Hey, Crocky, where are you going, man? This isn't the way to the lagoon."

Crocodile knew that he couldn't keep lying any longer. "I'm sorry, Monkey, but I lied to you. We aren't going to the lagoon."

"What do you mean? Why did you lie?" asked Monkey, starting to feel scared.

"We're going to my home, in the swamp."

"Why didn't you tell me we're going to your home? Are there more fruits there?" Monkey asked hopefully.

"No. There are no fruit trees there," said Crocodile, bursting to tell Monkey the truth. He was feeling very guilty about his secret plan even though it was to help his sick wife.

"Why did you tell me there was?" shrieked Monkey. He was starting to realize that he might be in serious trouble.

"I needed to trick you into getting on to my back." Crocodile's bulging eyes blinked slowly. He felt quite ashamed about what he was going to confess to Monkey.

"I don't understand. Why did you need me to get on to your back?" Monkey began pacing up and down on Crocodile's back, terrified of the answer.

"Oh dear. I feel very bad about this, Monkey, but you see, my wife is ill."

"I'm really sorry to hear that, Crocky. But what has that got to do with me?" Monkey was really worried now. From Crocodile's tone, somehow it was going to be bad news for him. He stood up straight on Crocodile's back, wishing he could just leap across to dry land.

By now they were entering the dark swamp with shadowy trees and mosquitoes buzzing around Monkey's head. Crocodile was very near his home and knew he'd have to tell Monkey the truth.

"Doctor Python examined her and said she has a rare illness. She can only be cured if she drinks a bowl of monkey liver soup. If I had told you the truth, I know you would not have come with me."

"MONKEY LIVER SOUP?" Monkey shouted. "You want my liver?" Monkey nearly slipped into the river from shock. He settled himself down and thought quickly. If he did not come up with a plan to get away from Crocodile quickly, he'd be made into soup. Pretending to be very friendly, he said, "Eh, eh, Crocky, man, you should have told me that you need my liver. I would happily give it to you, no problem."

Crocodile stopped moving. He couldn't believe his ears. "You'll give me your liver?" he asked in disbelief.

"Yes, of course. You didn't need to take me for a ride. I could have given it to you right by my tree."

"But why would you give me your liver, especially when I tried to trick you?" asked Crocodile suspiciously.

"You might have tried to trick me, but I can understand why. I'm sorry to hear about your wife, Crocky, and if I can help you both then I will." Monkey made his voice sympathetic. The only trouble is, you'll have to take me back to my tree to get it," said Monkey, gesturing back the way they had come.

"I don't understand. Why do we need to go back to your tree for your liver?" asked Crocodile.

"I don't have it on me. You see, I've not been feeling that great myself and so I went to see the doctor. He examined me and told me that I need to take my liver out and give it a good clean from time to time," explained Monkey seriously. "So that's what I did this morning. I took my liver out, cleaned it in the river and then I hung it out to dry on my balata tree. That's where I've left it."

Crocodile wasn't too sure about this explanation. "I didn't know you could take out your own liver," he said, confused.

"Of course, Crocky. Everybody does that. How do you think we monkeys stay so fit and lively?" Monkey was really trying to sound convincing.

"But don't you need your liver, Monkey?"

"No. Not at all. It's been giving me too much bother lately. I don't mind you having it. We will need to go back to my balata tree if you want me to get it for you," said Monkey.

"That's very kind of you. I really appreciate your help." said Crocodile, delighted that he was soon going to have the medicine he needed for his wife.

"Ah, anything for you, Crocky. I don't mind at all," beamed Monkey slyly.

Crocodile let out a huge sigh of relief. He had hated lying to Monkey. Slowly, he turned his heavy body around and glided back in the direction of the bay where he'd found Monkey. In no time at all, they reached the riverbank where the balata trees were. Crocodile swam to the water's edge and Monkey hopped off his back. He sprang up into the tree and started cracking open balata fruit and singing to himself about what a clever monkey he was.

"Monkey!" shouted Crocodile. "Hurry up, man, I haven't got all day. Bring down your liver."

"Ha!" cried Monkey. "There's no way I'm giving you my liver. It is safely tucked up inside of me and that's where it's going to stay until the day I die." Monkey turned and waved his pink bottom at Crocodile, laughing loudly at how gullible Crocodile was.

Crocodile knew that monkeys were clever tricksters and that he would have a tough job trying to cheat one. "I suppose I did try to trick you first, so that is fair," he sighed to himself. With a swish of his heavy tail, he turned away from the edge of the bank and swam back down the river, with Monkey's laughter echoing in his ears. He was feeling quite cross with himself at losing Monkey's liver, but he knew that he wasn't the best at playing tricks. Maybe another type of soup could help her feel better, he hoped.

Crocodile floated along the river as the sunlight faded away. He was wondering what he could make for their dinner when his nose picked up the scent of something quite spicy and delicious. He lifted his heavy body on to the riverbank, and followed the yummy smell which seemed to be coming from his home. He heard the sound of his wife humming and found her stirring a large pan of pepper pot stew.

"Mrs Crocky, what are you doing?" Crocodile asked. He was so surprised to see her up and looking so well. Her eyes were shining bright and she beamed at him.

"You're just in time for dinner. I'm feeling so much better after eating some of this spicy stew. It was just what I needed," she said cheerily.

Crocodile was so relieved. It turned out that pepper pot stew works just as well as monkey liver soup!

Kweku Anansi and the Unknown Challenge

Stories of Anansi the spider originate from the Ashanti people of Ghana, and variations are told all over the Caribbean. He is a clever, greedy rascal and in this tale, the king is so fed up with his boasting that he sets Anansi an impossible challenge.

There once was a wealthy and powerful king whose kingdom stretched along the western coast of Africa. His riches were so plentiful that his palace of ebony and stone was filled from floor to ceiling with golden armour and furniture. He dressed in the finest kente cloth with bright, bold shapes and wore the heaviest jewellery. Solid gold armbands and necklaces jingled together whenever he walked. Even his guards were exquisitely dressed with golden shields and swords.

While the king was known to be generous and fair to his people, he was consumed by thoughts of riches, particularly unusual, precious objects. His collection was filled with daggers set with jewels, golden face masks and fountains, but still he dreamed of three rare treasures that he wanted above all else: a pair of golden sandals which let your feet move with grace and speed, a golden plate and a golden cup which served up the tastiest food and drink. All of these magnificent golden treasures were owned by Death. Of course, the king knew that Death would eat any person who visited his house. So the king kept his secret wish for the sandals and cup to himself.

Kweku Anansi and his wife, Aso, also lived in

this kingdom. They were not wealthy, but always had enough, thanks to Anansi's wisdom and cunning. He was known to be so clever and wise that even the king's advisors would ask for his help. Despite being loved by his people, the king was jealous of Anansi's wisdom and popularity. And on the other hand, Kweku Anansi was jealous of the king's power and wealth. He was fed up with only having wisdom. He wanted more. He wanted riches beyond his imagination, so one day, he decided to do something about it.

Forming a plan, Anansi went to the busy market. He saw a large crowd near the basket sellers. *This is a good place to be seen and heard*, he thought to himself, and stood under a bright red umbrella which would give him shade and make him stand out in the crowd. As soon as he saw the king's advisors passing by, Anansi put his plan into action and started boasting very loudly.

"I am so wise, everyone comes to me if they have a problem." Anansi raised his voice louder when he saw one of the advisors listening.

"I am so clever, I could get anything for the king without the king even telling me *what* it is he wants!" Anansi puffed up his chest and carried on bragging about his wisdom and skill all afternoon.

During a council meeting, one of the king's advisors mentioned Anansi's boasting to the king.

"Kweku Anansi was in the market today, boasting loudly about how he is so wise he knows what you want without you even telling him," he said as they all sat around the king's golden throne.

"Yes, it is true," said another advisor. "I even heard him say he is wiser than the king himself!"

When the king heard this, he was furious and slammed his fist down on the council table. "How dare that rascal compare himself to me!" he yelled. He turned to one of his guards and said, "Bring Kweku Anansi to me right now."

Anansi appeared before the king. He bowed his head respectfully and glanced at all the golden ornaments hanging around the room. He smiled slyly to himself. His plan to gain more riches was working. He knew that the king would test his boasts and he was confident that, using his trickster ways, he would be able to deliver what the king wanted. The king glared down from his throne, boring holes into the back of Anansi's head with his eyes.

"You think you are more clever than me, Kweku

Anansi?" asked the king, his voice blazing with fury.

Anansi knelt down and bowed his head even lower, almost touching the floor.

"Oh no, my king, I was only offering my services to you. I want to prove myself to you – give me a task, any task at all, and I will complete it for you."

The king thought of an idea to get rid of Anansi. "Fine. If you are so wise, I will set you a challenge. There is something I want you to get for me, but I won't tell you what it is. Only my trusted advisors will know. If you complete the challenge within one week, you can take away as many of my riches as you are able to carry. If you fail and do not complete the challenge, you will be put to death for your boasting." The king thought this was an impossible challenge, but to his surprise, Anansi accepted.

"Of course, my king. Whatever you want, I will do." He shuffled out of the room without turning his back on the king so as to show how much he respected him. Once he was alone, the king laughed to himself. *That boastful Anansi will fail, and even if he does succeed, Death will surely eat him. Either way, I will be rid of Kweku Anansi and his awful boasting.*

Anansi strolled into the forest, feeling rather pleased with himself. He was not worried at all. Many people owed Anansi a favour for all the advice and help he had given them over the years. He knew that his friends would help him to find out exactly what the king secretly wanted. Still smiling, he entered the kingdom of birds in the centre of the forest, where the most colourful birds lived. Twittering bird melodies sprinkled through the trees.

Tut tut tut tut
Loooooo, looooooo
Cricccccck, criccccccck
Craaaaaaaack, craaaaaack

Magenta sunbirds sipped sweet nectar from flowers. Hornbills crushed dark berries with their long orange beaks. Anansi looked up into the canopy of trees and called out to the birds.

"My friends, I am on a very important mission for the king. It is so top secret that I cannot tell you what it is. But I need your help." The birds peeped out from behind the leaves, spread their wings and flew down from their branches to listen to him.

The golden firebird, with her bright fiery feathers, spoke first.

"You have helped us all when we needed any advice. Tell us what you need, Kweku Anansi, and we will help you," she said, spreading her yellow wings out wide.

"Thank you, golden firebird," said Anansi. "I need one feather from each of you. I need enough to cover me from head to toe for a disguise," he explained. The birds all agreed and gave Anansi one of their feathers for his secret mission. Anansi rushed back home to his wife, Aso, and asked her to help glue the feathers all over his body. She shook her head in dismay and wondered what trick Anansi was getting up to now. But together they stuck feathers of all colours and sizes on his head, arms, legs and feet. Every part of Anansi's body was covered except for his face. He had so many feathers that when he waved his arms up and down, his feet lifted right off the ground. "I can fly!" he cried, and jumped about flapping his long arms like a bird. After a bit of practice, Anansi found that he could lift his whole body off the ground and soar like a bird. With his arms spread out, he flew all the way over to the palace to find out what challenge the king had set for him. He perched on the branch of a tall baobab tree in the courtyard. Down below, the king was sitting with advisors, discussing royal business. The king suddenly caught sight of a large colourful bird in the tree, with feathers the full spectrum of the rainbow.

"Look at that amazing bird!" he cried to his advisors. "What vibrant feathers," he marvelled. Anansi swivelled around in the tree, showing off his long tail and the spiky crown of feathers on his head. The king walked towards the tree for a closer look.

"What is the name of this magnificent bird?" he asked them, but they all shook their heads and shrugged. No one had ever seen such a colourful bird before. Anansi puffed up his chest, which shone a metallic blue in the sunshine.

"Arrrgh," fumed the king. "What a shame I have already given Anansi the challenge of getting me the golden slippers, plate and cup from Death. He would have captured this bird for me and told me its name." His voice carried up into the trees, loud enough for Anansi to hear. Delighted his plan had worked, he fluttered his bright wings, just as the king started to speak again. "I want that bird for my collection.

Capture it for me now," he ordered. Two of the advisors jumped up from their seats and prepared to climb the tree and grab the colourful bird. But Anansi was far too swift. He fluttered his bright wings again and flew straight home. With Aso's help, he removed all of his beautiful feathers and kept them in case he needed to disguise himself again.

"My wife, please prepare a hearty meal for me. I have to make a dangerous, perilous journey to the house of Death," Anansi told Aso. "I am going on a very important mission to steal something for the king."

"What madness is this, Anansi? You know that you cannot steal from Death. He will kill you," Aso said. She tutted, but knew that his mind was made up. Resigned, Aso did as Anansi asked and cooked a meal for his journey. She prepared *waakye*, rice and beans with *kelewele,* spicy fried plantains, wrapped them in banana leaves and placed them in a cloth for Anansi to take with him. The next morning before the sun grew too hot, Anansi set off for the house of Death. He knew that no one had ever returned from there to tell their tale, but he did not let that bother him. *I am Kweku Anansi, the clever trickster,* he thought, and he felt confident that he could outwit Death.

He made his way out of the village and across the valley of darkness where the black crows and eagles scavenged. He walked all day across the dry plains with the sun beating down upon his head until he came to a small forest, thick with trees. He entered as the sun was starting to dip beneath the trees and realized he was feeling quite hungry. He stopped by a flowing stream and sat on a log to eat some of the delicious food that Aso had packed. As he bit into his *waakye*, the stream smelled the food and gently called out to him.

"Kweku Anansi, please give me some of your food. I would love to try some."

Anansi was not keen on sharing his food at first, but his clever mind thought that it was worth doing, as then the stream would owe him a favour. And favours were always worth having.

"I'll give you some of my food," he said, "but if I return this way, you must promise to help me." The stream agreed and Anansi threw some of his meal into the water before carrying on with his journey. It was evening time now and the sun had completely disappeared. In the darkness, Anansi felt something crawling up his legs. "OUCH!" he yelled, hopping up and down. Something had bitten his toes. He looked down and saw a group of red fire ants scurrying around on the ground. They were hungry and had smelled his food, just like the stream.

"Sorry, Kweku Anansi," they squeaked. "We are hungry. Please share some of your food with us." Again Anansi was not keen on giving away any of his food, but again he offered it to them on one condition.

"I will give you some food if you promise to watch out for me here tomorrow. Help me if I pass this way." The fire ants happily agreed and gobbled up the crumbs which Anansi sprinkled on the ground for them.

Anansi was feeling quite tired now and wondered how much further he would need to walk until he found the house of Death. He had been walking all day and he began to grumble to himself, wishing he was in his comfortable bed at home.

"Why did I take on this difficult challenge? I wish I was tucked up in bed."

"Well, that can be arranged, Kweku Anansi." A cold, steely voice spoke out in the pitch-black darkness. Anansi spun around and tried to see who was there. But even as he glanced wildly about, he knew deep inside it was the voice of Death. Anansi felt his stomach lurch as he laid eyes on Death. He had been so fearless before, but now his confidence was a little shaken. Death's grey eyes blinked slowly in the darkness. He lifted his long arm and pushed back the trees, revealing his tall, windowless house. But rather than being scary, Death was pleased to see Anansi. No one ever visited him unless they were lost or banished, and he was starting to become hungry. He welcomed Anansi into his home with a broad smile.

"Come and rest. You must be tired after your long journey, Kweku Anansi," Death said sweetly. He led Anansi down a dimly lit corridor and opened the door to a room. Inside was a low bed, covered with plump, fluffy pillows.

"Make yourself comfortable, Kweku Anansi. Get a wonderful night's rest and then tomorrow we shall feast together," said Death, his stomach rumbling as he imagined all the ways he could eat Anansi. He closed the door and quietly disappeared along the corridor to wait for Anansi to fall asleep so that he could sneak back in and eat him.

Anansi sat on the bed and listened in the darkness to every single sound. He was no fool. He knew Death had a trick or two up his sleeve. But Anansi the trickster was ready for him.

Whoooooosh. Whoooooooosh. Whip, whip. The wind howled outside, stirring the leaves.

Tip tap, tip tap, tip tap, tip tap. Rats scampered across the thatched roof.

Chirrup, chirrup. Scrape, scrape. Crickets and bats scratched against the bamboo walls.

Anansi twitched at every sound. He sat with eyes WIDE open, determined not to fall asleep. After a while, Death came to eat Anansi. He slowly turned the handle of his bedroom door. He walked up to the bed and there in the middle of the room, in the middle of the night, sat Kweku Anansi with his eyes WIDE open, determined not to fall asleep.

"Why are you not asleep?" asked Death, feeling cross that he could not eat Anansi as he'd planned.

"Oh, I find it really hard to get to sleep without my golden sandals. Do you have a pair that I can borrow?" asked the trickster Anansi. Death thought it was a bit unusual to need golden sandals at bedtime, but he did not mind lending his ones if it meant he could eat Anansi sooner. He fetched his golden sandals, gave them to Anansi and left him to sleep. But now the hour was late, and Death found himself tired. He decided he would eat Anansi tomorrow.

At sunrise, the black crows gathered outside, squawking to start the day. Anansi found Death preparing a delicious breakfast. The table was laid out with *kooko* porridge, sugar bread, fritters and lots of fruits. But instead of tucking into the food, Anansi sat in silence.

"What is the matter, Kweku Anansi? Why are you not eating and drinking?" Death asked, hoping to fatten Anansi up before he ate him later.

"I'm so sorry, Death. Everything looks very tasty, but I can only eat and drink from a golden plate and cup. I left mine at home, may I borrow yours?"

Death was surprised at Anansi's request but did not mind lending his, still dreaming of how tasty Anansi was going to be. He fetched his golden cup and poured Anansi some water. Anansi ate and ate, filling his stomach with all of the yummy food. Then he asked Death if he could help himself to some water from the kitchen. Death nodded and watched Anansi stroll out of the room to fetch some water. He did not notice Anansi walk past the kitchen and out of the house. Anansi kept walking right into the forest and then he began to run. His feet were flying with speed, wearing Death's golden sandals, carrying the golden plate and cup in his hand, heading for home.

After a while, Death wondered what was taking Anansi so long to come back. He called out to him, "Is everything all right, Anansi? You are taking a long time." When he heard no reply from the kitchen, Death started to feel a little anxious. He hurried into the kitchen and saw that his fears had come true. Anansi had disappeared. Death quickly looked around his house, searching high and low, hoping that Anansi was being nosy and simply looking around his home. He reached for his golden sandals which would carry him swiftly, and saw that Anansi had left with them. And then he realized that the clever trickster had run off with his golden plate and cup, too! Death's eyes nearly popped out of his head and he howled out loud with rage. "ANANSIIIIIII!" His tummy turned somersaults and croaked with hunger. He was so looking forward to eating Anansi and now he had fled. Death wasted no time and flew out of his house, all the doors slamming shut with his fury.

Death moved swiftly through the forest after Anansi, who was running as fast as he could.

Anansi, gasping for breath, called out to the red fire ants as he passed them.

"Remember you owe me a favour! Help me to slow Death down!" The ants remembered their promise to Anansi and swarmed around on the ground, waiting. When Death approached, they scampered up his legs, crawling all over Death's body, tickling him so much that he could not move. It took Death quite some time to brush the red fire ants off and carry on his chase of Anansi.

By now, Anansi had reached the stream. Huffing and puffing from running so far, he called out, "Remember you owe me a favour! Please help me to slow Death down." The stream told Anansi to jump in and she moved her current faster, pushing him towards his village.

By the time Death reached the stream, she had turned into a deep river which overflowed on to the banks. Her current was swirling and twirling like a giant whirlpool. Death tried to step in but he knew that he could not cross such treacherous water. The current was moving too fast. He would have to turn back.

"Kweku Anansi, you have robbed me of my treasures!" Death screamed out into the sky with anger, startling all of the birds from their trees. The sky grew dark and cloudy with Death's stormy outburst. Anansi had gotten the best of him today, but Death would not be tricked again so easily. With one swish of his black robes, Death turned around and went back home, promising that he would find Anansi one day soon.

Safely back in his village, Anansi went home and rested for a while. He bathed and changed into fresh clothes. Then he ate dinner with his wife, Aso, and told her about his adventures. He wrapped the golden sandals and golden cup into a brightly coloured cloth and strolled over to the king's palace. The king was surprised to see him and overjoyed when Anansi presented the golden treasures from the house of Death.

"You are indeed very wise, Kweku Anansi, and you shall have your reward," said the king. "I will lead you to my room of treasures, where you can take as many precious gifts as you can carry."

Anansi's eyes shone with happiness, thinking of how he could pile up lots of treasures into his bag and drag them out of the palace. Just before he let Anansi go wild with his treasures, the king asked him to solve one more problem.

"I saw a multicoloured bird in my baobab tree. Its tail was flowing long and its crest of feathers stood up like a crown. Tell me the name of this bird and you shall collect your reward."

Anansi the trickster smiled broadly. Instead of telling the king it was him in disguise, he made up a name and bragged, "Oh, *that* bird! I know it well. It has a very long name – *wosuro asententena, wonte mpaninsem* – which means 'you need patience to hear wisdom'."

"Ah," said the king, nodding thoughtfully. "If I am more patient, I could gain more wisdom as a king." Anansi strolled off laden with his piles of gold, laughing to himself. After all, it was patience and wisdom that helped him trick both the king and Death.

Magic And Mystery

The stories in this section are tales of characters who have found themselves in difficult situations filled with conflict they need to overcome. Mysterious forces flow through the stories in the shape of Caribbean spirits and powerful African gods. A magical tree saves a child, the gods punish an entire village, a greedy leopard is served justice and an old lady tries to cheat death.

The Orange Tree

(Haiti)

This story is a Creole folktale which originates from the Caribbean country of Haiti, on the island of Hispaniola. It is about a young boy who steals from a wicked old man and magically creates an orange tree to escape the old man's wrath.

There once was a mean old man who lived on a huge farm. His fields were filled with golden corn, cassava, sweet potatoes and yams. Too old and too mean to look after the farm himself, he let orphans live there in exchange for work on the farm. Crooked by height with his back bent double and crooked by nature with a heart made of stone, the old man fed the orphans very little and paid them even less. They would scrub, sweep and dig until their fingers bled and their hollow tummies cried out for food.

One of the boys, Ti, was tall and thin, his limbs hanging long like the twigs of a tree. Like the rest of the orphans, he was always hungry and on the lookout for food. One day, when the old man hobbled into town, Ti spied three oranges nestled in a bowl on the kitchen table. Aglow with sunlit colour, their bittersweet smell filled the room. He moved closer and sniffed. He could almost taste their sharpness.

"No one will miss one," he said to himself as his fingers peeled off its stippled skin. "No one will miss two," he muttered, taking another, swallowing the flesh from each piece before he could even chew.

When only one orange was left in the bowl, Ti

scratched his head and thought, *Oh no, what will the old man do? What will he say?* But hunger knows no shame and so he quickly gobbled the last of the three oranges.

When the old man returned and saw that his oranges were missing, he was purple with rage.

"Who stole my oranges?" he bellowed, swinging his walking stick from side to side like a club. "Tell me right now or I'll skin you from head to toe." His dark eyes pierced each child as they scattered like mice into every corner.

Terrified, Ti ran out of the house and across the cornfield. He made his way to the cemetery where his mother was buried. He found her tombstone of jagged rocks and lay beside her grave.

"Mama, won't you help me? I'm in lots of trouble. All because I ate some oranges," he wept.

As the day stretched into night, the nocturnal creatures kept watch. Tiny frogs sat frozen on the leaves, their red eyes squinting in the darkness. A giant black cloud of bats spread their wings and screeched across the sky. The forest was awake and listening. An orange seed fell from Ti's clothes on to the ground.

Ti continued to cry, and his tears soaked the earth

and watered the seed. The seed began to swell and grow. It first grew roots and the roots took hold. Out from the earth popped a green shoot. When Ti saw this new tree sprouting from the ground, he was filled with hope. He wiped away his tears and began to sing.

Grow, orange tree, grow.
Grow, orange tree, grow.

The tree twisted and turned to face the morning sun. Ti continued to sing:

Grow more, orange tree, grow more.
Grow more, orange tree, grow more.

White flowers appeared on the branches as the tree grew taller, and Ti continued to sing:

Blossom, orange tree, blossom.
Blossom, orange tree, blossom.

The flowers bloomed and small green oranges glistened beside them, and still Ti sang:

Grow ripe, orange tree, grow ripe.
Grow ripe, orange tree, grow ripe.

Ti lifted his head up high as the tree sailed past him. The oranges turned golden as the sun greeted each one. He was overjoyed that now he could replace the oranges he'd stolen from the old man! He stretched up to pluck three oranges from the tree but the branches were too high and so he sang again:

Bend, orange tree, bend.
Bend, orange tree, bend.

Ti stretched out his arms as the tree lowered its branches. He picked as many oranges as he could and ran quickly back to the farm. The old man sat hunched over a stool, snoozing outside his barn. Ti tiptoed past him, carrying an armful of the sweet oranges. The other children squealed with delight when he gave them each an orange to eat. They sat huddled together, filling their empty tummies, before Ti remembered the ones he had stolen from the old man.

He went back to the bowl on the kitchen table

and placed three oranges there. Just as he was about to leave, a long brown stick slammed down on the table, narrowly missing his small fingers.

"Where did these oranges come from?" yelled the old man.

Ti shrank back and stammered in reply: "I-I found an orange tree. You were so angry that your oranges were gone, so I picked some new ones for you to eat."

The old man grabbed an orange from the bowl and roughly peeled its soft, dappled skin. He stuffed the whole orange into his mouth and was startled by its delicious flavour. It was the most exquisite orange he had ever eaten. He grabbed Ti by his shirt collar and pulled him close to his snarling face.

"Show me where you got these oranges from, boy."

Ti's eyes rattled around his head as the old man shook him. "I don't know if I can find the exact place again," he replied, trying to pull away from the old man's grasp.

"Take me there right now," he demanded. "Or I'll lock all of you in the cellar for a week."

Ti had no choice but to lead the old man to the orange tree. By this time, the tree had doubled in size, its branches leaping out towards the sky.

The old man's eyes widened with amazement at the sight of the ripe oranges, nestled between the leaves. He calculated all the money he could make from selling fruit from this magical tree.

"Climb up and get me those oranges," he said, pushing Ti towards the tree.

Ti looked up and began to sing:

Bend, orange tree, bend.
Bend, orange tree, bend.

With a whisper of magic stirring between its branches, the orange tree began to bend towards the little boy. He reached up and pulled an orange from its branch.

The old man snatched and devoured the orange, marvelling again at the sweet, tangy taste.

"I'm going to climb the tree myself and get all of those oranges," he cried. He let go of his walking stick and climbed on to the lowest branch, inching towards the fruit. He grabbed another orange and ripped into the flesh, swallowing the pieces without even chewing. He reached further into the tree, stretching and climbing zealously.

Ti watched from below and wondered if he could

get rid of the old man by leaving him so high up in the tree that he would never be able to get down. He began to sing:

Grow, orange tree, grow.
Grow orange tree, grow.

The tree obeyed his command and grew higher still, towering above any other tree. Its branches swayed with the weight of its fruit and the old man clung on, grabbing at the oranges.

Rise, orange tree, rise.
Rise, orange tree, rise

Ti sang until he could no longer see the top of the tree. It grew to a tremendous height, shattering the clouds which lay sleepily in the sky. The old man remained up there for ever, greedily eating his oranges. Ti felt pity for the mean old man, but was also very happy that he was gone and never coming back. The children were now free to run the farm as they pleased and enjoy the rewards of their hard work. The farm blossomed from their care, with golden bananas hanging from trees and fields swaying with yellow corn. Whenever they needed oranges to sell, Ti would visit the magical tree and sing loud and clear into its branches:

Bend, orange tree, bend.
Bend, orange tree, bend.

And the tree would twist and curl, lowering its arms for Ti to reach and pick the sweetest oranges you'll ever taste on the island.

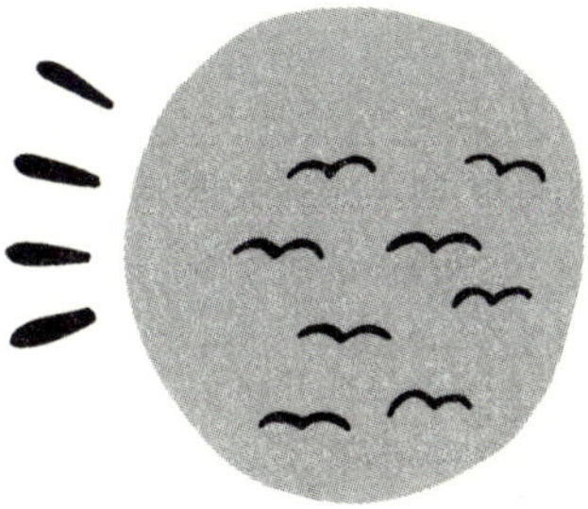

The Prince Who Wanted the Moon

(THE CONGO)

This is a "pourquoi" story from the Democratic Republic of the Congo. Pourquoi stories are origin stories that explain how things came to be, such as why the zebra has no horns or why a snake has no legs. This story explains how birds came to be in the world – all because of a spoilt young prince and how he angered the gods.

A long, long time ago, there lived a very wealthy king. His kingdom stretched across the golden coast of West Africa. He was known to be a fair and wise ruler by his people, who loved him. But the king had one weakness – he couldn't say no to his only son. The young prince was nearly ten years old, and his father doted on him and gave him everything he ever wanted.

The prince had only to snap his fingers or nod his head before his every request was granted. If he was hungry, a lavish banquet of food would be laid out for him. If he did not feel like walking, he would stretch out his arms and a throne carved from exquisite wenge wood would be placed beneath him. He was lifted up high and carried wherever he wanted to go. The prince even had his own palace filled with opulent treasures and magnificent clothes.

You would think the prince would be the happiest child in the whole of the world. But despite all of this luxury, the prince was never satisfied. Whatever he was given, he always found something to complain about.

One bright, sunny morning, he turned to his father the king and said, "Father, I am bored.

I would like to rule over my sisters so that I can practise for when I am king."

The king looked horrified. He imagined his daughters complaining to him about their brother being in charge of them.

"No, my son. It is not right for your sisters to be ordered around by their brother. It does not seem just or fair." The king hoped that would be the end of the conversation, but the prince was not willing to hear the word no.

"Father, there must be a way to make it fair. After all, it will happen one day when I am king." He smirked at his reply, thinking that he had cornered his father and would soon have his way. He stood with his hands on his hips and his nose in the air, trying to pose like a ruler. The king sighed deeply and realized his son would not give up. He admired his son's tenacity and thought perhaps there could be another way.

"Rather than ruling over just your sisters, I will give you the power to rule over all of the children in the kingdom. Then everyone will be dealt equal justice." He made his voice firm to signal this was his last offer and the prince bowed his head to signal that he agreed.

The young prince was given a special conch shell which he used to call the children to him. Whenever they heard the sound of the horn from the conch, they had to stop whatever they were doing and rush to the prince's side.

Every day the prince summoned all of the children in the kingdom and made up new laws for them to obey. They had to sit very still in silence and listen to whatever he commanded. The prince loved showing off and having an audience. Rather than ordering them to do exciting things to help their village, he preferred to make them follow him around. Most of his requests were very dull for the children.

"Today you shall watch me as I take an afternoon nap," he ordered.

"Now you must watch me eat my lunch," he snapped.

"Everyone must cheer for me whenever I walk past," he demanded.

This went on for several days, and then weeks, and soon life was quite dull for the children in the kingdom. Instead of helping their parents to fetch water down by the river, weaving or playing games under the shadows of the giant trees, they were watching the prince perform his daily rituals for no reason.

One afternoon, they sat watching him being fed his meal of liboké wild leaves filled with boiled vegetables. They were not allowed to leave until he gave permission. He finished his food and stood with his hands on his hips. His gold bracelets sparkled around each wrist and he caught one of the children staring at his jewellery in awe. He could have offered it to the child, as he had so many, but instead he strutted around like a proud peacock and announced with his nose in the air: "I am the greatest prince in the land. I can have anything I want."

Suddenly he heard a voice ring out from the crowd of children.

"I know something you can't have."

The prince sprung around and tried to see where the voice had come from. Everyone sat very still on the dusty ground, with their heads bowed and faces as solemn as midnight.

"Who said that?" he shrieked, shocked that someone would disagree with him.

"I know something you can't have," sang a girl's mocking voice again.

"Name it. Name one thing I can't have!" yelled the prince, searching for the voice among the rows of curly black hair all bowed low before him.

A girl named Ivarem stood up at the back. She faced the prince, with her arms crossed and her dark eyes narrowed like a cat about to pounce. She was fed up with the prince's boasting and foolish commands. She would much rather be swimming in the river or playing tug of war with her friends. She had had enough. It was time to make the foolish prince see that he was no better than anyone else.

"You don't have the moon in the sky," she said in a lofty voice, and pointed to the sky. Her lips curled into a sneer. "It's been placed there by the gods for us all to enjoy. YOU don't have and YOU can't get it." The golden thread weaving through her braids shimmered in the sunlight as she held her head high.

The prince could not think of a single reply. It was true. He did not have the moon and he couldn't think of a way to get it.

All the children lifted their heads and burst out laughing. They held their sides and fell about on the ground, as their laughter echoed all around them. The prince was very embarrassed. He'd never been laughed at before by anyone and he hated being told he couldn't have something he wanted. He stormed off to the palace in a huff and went straight to his father, the king.

"Father, I want you to get me the moon," he demanded. "I am the prince and I should have the moon."

The king looked down at his son in amusement, thinking he was playing a game. He patted him gently on his head and dismissed him.

"I am serious," said the prince as his father turned away. "I want to have the moon." He tugged at the king's long raffia skirt. "If you do not get me the moon, I will make myself sick. I will not eat. I will not sleep and I will not talk to anyone."

The king was horrified at this idea. He loved his son very much and did not want him to be ill. His face softened as he tried to explain why it was a terrible idea.

"My son, this request is far too great. The moon is not there for us to give or take; it does not belong to us," he said calmly, hoping his son would understand. But he did not. The prince twisted his mouth into an ugly shape and spat out his next words.

"Nothing should be too great for a KING! How pitiful that you will not rise to the challenge." His words pierced his father's heart, leaving a throbbing wound. The prince stamped his feet and spoke through gritted teeth. "What will the gods think of you if you deny your son his only wish?"

The king was shocked at the scorn in his son's voice. He knew that it was a ridiculous idea, but he wanted to impress him and fulfil his wish.

"Leave it with me. I will come up with a plan. You shall have your wish," said the king softly.

Later that evening, the king summoned his council of wise advisors.

"I want you to find a way to get my son the moon," he said gravely.

The advisors were shocked into silence. They stood staring at the feet, not wanting the king to see the fear in their eyes. How could they achieve such an impossible task? they all thought.

Finally one of them spoke up. "My king, we do not think this is a good idea. The moon belongs to the gods and we may incur their wrath if we remove it from the sky." He bowed his head respectfully as he spoke and hoped that the king would be discouraged by the threat of punishment from the gods.

The king knew that his advisors were right, but he did not care. Despite always being respectful to the gods, he was now only thinking of making his son happy. He refused to face his son without good news.

"My only son has made this request and you must find a way to solve it," he ordered his advisors, and sent them away to come up with a solution.

The advisors gathered together that night in their special hut for meetings. A circle of moonlight streamed in from their open thatched roof. They sat around a glowing fire and disagreed among themselves over whether to try to do what the king wanted or serve the gods, leaving the moon where they had put it.

"Maybe the prince will forget about his idea? We should wait and see what happens," said one advisor, rubbing his hands together and warming them by the fire.

"If we wait, the king will grow impatient. He will punish us, I'm sure," said another.

"Better he punish us than the gods!" they all agreed, nodding wisely.

They spent the next few days together, meeting in their hut, coming up with ideas which would allow the prince to reach the moon while not angering the gods.

"We can lead him to the highest mountain where he will be closer to the moon."

"Why not tie him to our largest eagle? He can soar high into the sky, towards the moon."

"Let us advise him to visit the river at night. He can stand on the bank and look across the rippled water to gaze upon the silvery reflection of the moon."

None of the ideas seemed quite good enough, but finally they all agreed on a plan to present to the king.

Early one morning, under the shade of the giant baobab tree, the advisors sat with the king to tell him their solution.

"My king, you must bring all of your strongest champions and get them to build a tower from the most durable trees. They will need to spend many years chopping, gathering and constructing a frame that will loom high into the sky. Once it has been built, the prince can climb the tower and reach out to touch the moon."

The king thought this was a good idea, and he arranged for work to begin immediately. Over the next ten years, the wise people of the kingdom hoped that the prince would forget about his request to have the moon, but he did not. He called upon the children in the kingdom every day so that they could watch the tower being built. He turned to Ivarem one day and said in a mocking tone, "I have you to thank for this wonderful gift. Soon I shall have the moon." But she merely shook her head in pity at his arrogance and pleaded with him.

"You don't need to prove how powerful you are. Please stop this impossible challenge. It is our village that will suffer just to satisfy your greed."

But the prince was used to getting everything that he wanted and refused to believe there was anything he could not own. The warriors chopped ancient trees, gathered all the wood and built this colossal tower, moving closer and closer towards the moon. The villagers were unsure at first but soon became impressed with the mighty tower that rose higher and higher above their homes, trees and mountaintops. The gods looked on from above without intervening, hoping that the people would come to their senses. But instead the villagers held celebrations to congratulate their prince. They sang and danced, marvelling as the tower pushed through the clouds. They built plank after plank, year after year, watching it grow higher and higher until it was finally complete.

One morning, as dawn splashed her rosy colours across the sky, the wise advisors announced to the king and his son that the tower was ready to climb. They were so relieved that the building work was at last over. Now they could get back to normal life and start repairing the forests. The arrogant prince, who was now a young man, barely thanked the advisors and warriors, saying, "At last it is completed. You have kept me waiting long enough." He was eager to start climbing and could not wait to begin. The king beamed with pride and said, "My son, you will be the first prince to reach the moon." He had not given any thought to the journey they had to make.

There was a frenzy of excitement moving through the village as word soon spread.

The Tower is finished. The Tower is finished. We have reached the moon!

The prince gathered everyone in the kingdom to accompany him on his journey to the moon. Only the girl Ivarem and her family refused to go with them. She watched from her bedroom window, as other villagers spoke excitedly about their journey to the moon. Many were curious about what lay ahead and wondered what it would be like to climb higher than the birds. Ivarem shook her head, muttering, "The gods will not like this. The moon should stay in the sky."

They climbed all day and they climbed all night. One by one they followed the king and the prince until they reached the very peak of the tower.

They hung in the stillness of the night air, waiting for the luminous moon to glide over their heads. Before long, iridescent clouds of dust floated away and the moon drifted over their heads.

The king was amazed at the beauty of the moon. He stared in wonder as a bright, warm glow shimmered all around them. The prince also felt the warmth and hung back, letting his father go first. The king reached out with his fingertips to touch the moon and yelled out in pain. "OWWWW," he cried, trying to soothe his hand. "The moon is blazing hot. You must not touch it, my son."

But the king was trying to advise a prince who had never taken no for an answer before in his life.

"I have been waiting for many years to have the moon. You are not going to stop me. I want it," he yelled, and he pushed past his father roughly, not caring if his father burned himself.

The prince stretched up to catch hold of the moon and large bits of moon rock crumbled off in his hand. At first he felt triumphant at having the moon in his grasp, but that soon turned to terror as a scorching pain surged through his body. His hand began to burn.

Blistering hot moon rock scorched the prince and fell on to the tower, causing it to burst into flames. The people screamed out as the fire spread rapidly along the wooden frame. The people plummeted towards the earth as the flames engulfed the tower.

The African gods looked on from their timeless place in the sky and shook their heads in pity. "Look at these foolish people," they said sadly, knowing that everyone would die if they did not help them. "Leave them to their fate, it is what they deserve," said one god, but others disagreed, saying, "Let us be merciful and let them live."

Whilst the gods debated on which direction to take, the people continued to tumble down towards their deaths. Far down below, Ivarem rushed outside when she heard the cries coming from the sky. She watched through her fingers, fearing the worst.

After much grumbling, the gods made up their minds. They would save their people. The gods reached through the clouds and caught each person in the palm of their hands. The terrifying screams gradually stopped as people landed softly, realizing that they were somehow still alive.

"Thank the gods, thank the gods!" many of them called out, cheering and crying with happiness. A flash of sunlight suddenly streaked across the sky. Ivarem heard the joyful voices change and suddenly she could not understand their words.

"Caaaawwwww, cawwwww, croooooak," was all she could hear coming from up above. Ivarem looked up and saw the gods transform all of the villagers into colourful birds with light feathery wings and long thin beaks. They flipped and flopped, darting across the sky. The gods had saved their lives but also punished them for daring to believe they could own the moon in the sky.

From that day on Ivarem often told the story of the prince who wanted the moon. She shared the story of how the gods took pity on the people, despite their foolishness, pointing to the sky above at the swooping birds – warning the African people not to repeat their prince's mistake.

That is why still to this day, if you look up in the sky, you can see magnificent birds soaring high, but not high enough to reach the moon.

Why the Leopard Has Spots

(GHANA)

This story is a wonderful folktale that is told in a variety of ways across Africa. This version originates from the Ashanti people of Ghana in West Africa. These stories are filled with wisdom and humour where a main character, in this case the leopard, is taught a meaningful life lesson.

There once was a time when Leopard had no spots. His fur was many shades of chestnut brown, which helped him to blend into the colours of the forest. He would silently come and go without being noticed and he loved his cloak of invisibility.

One year, there was a drought across the land and food was scarce. All summer, crops had been drying up in the blazing heat. Some of the animals had been wise and carefully stored up food to celebrate the harvest. Leopard had been lazy, preferring to let others do the hard work.

On the day of the Harvest Festival, everyone was looking forward to a huge feast that was held every year in the middle of the forest. There was to be a long procession of all the animals marching, singing and dancing their way into the forest with Lion leading the way. A firepit had been dug and yams had been laid out for everyone to celebrate and eat. As they made their way along, Leopard quietly walked behind. He didn't feel much like singing and he certainly wasn't in the mood for dancing. In fact, all he wanted to do was eat. He hadn't had much luck finding food during the drought and hadn't eaten for days. He knew he wouldn't get any food until the end of the procession. How he wished the animals would just hurry up, instead of stopping to dance.

Everyone else was feeling great and having a wild time. Monkey was riding on Elephant's back and singing loudly, while Lizard scurried along behind Snake. Leopard just watched them miserably, his tummy rumbling. Finally, all the animals reached the middle of the forest and Lion let out a loud roar for everyone to form a circle so the dancing could continue.

As Leopard hung back, feeling too grumpy to join in, the earthy smell of roasted yams drifted towards him. *Oooh, the yams must be nearby*, thought Leopard hungrily, and decided to take a look. Blending into the trees with his light brown fur, Leopard wandered off into the forest with his nose in the air. He followed the scent, sniffing the ground until he came across the roots of a giant fig tree. Piled up high at the foot of the tree were the roasted yams for the harvest feast. There were so many yams and they smelled delicious. Leopard licked his lips longingly. He couldn't resist taking one to eat. *No one will miss one*, he thought, looking around to see if anyone was watching. With his brown fur, he blended into the forest and no one saw him grabbing a yam between his jaws. It was delicious. *I'll just have one more*, he thought, convincing himself to take another. This one was even more tasty than the last one. *There's way too much here for everyone, I'll just have a few more and then I'll stop.* Without even realizing it, he carried on eating. Before long he'd swallowed every single yam and his tummy was full. Leopard stared in horror at the empty space on the ground which had just been full of yams. He felt very guilty, but it was too late. The yams were all gone. He was too ashamed to tell anyone his secret, so he quickly joined the other animals and pretended he had been watching the dancing all the time.

Soon the dancing reached a peak and it was time to relax and share in the harvested yams. Lion went to the feasting area and frowned, seeing that it was empty of yams. He wondered if he had the wrong spot. He walked a little further, thinking that all that dancing had made him tired and forgetful. Still he found no yams, and so he asked Zebra for help.

"Zebra, where did you put all of the yams? I thought your herd had carried them here?" She scowled and replied, "Of course we did, they are in the clearing behind where we were dancing." Zebra entered the place where the yams had been piled and saw that it was empty. She spun around in anger and began to bark loudly. The other zebras came in answer to her call. They stood in shock, staring at where they had left the yams. "Someone must have taken them," piped a voice from the back of the crowd. When he heard the voice, Lion let out a loud roar which bellowed through the canopy of trees.

"Who has eaten all of our yams? Which one of you has done this?"

All the animals looked at each other, shaking their heads in disbelief, murmuring their surprise. Leopard blended into the undergrowth of the forest with his chestnut-brown fur. He hid in plain sight, hoping that no one would see the guilt on his face. Everyone stared suspiciously at their neighbours, wondering who the thief was and feeling cross at being accused of such an act.

"I was looking forward to sinking my teeth into some sweet yams," moaned Hyena, his mouth watering as he spoke.

"I definitely didn't eat the yams. The entire forest would have seen me and my stripes," huffed Zebra, shaking her dark mane indignantly. Leopard was starting to feel a bit sick. Perhaps it was because he had eaten too many yams, or maybe it was because he regretted what he had done.

"Everyone knows where I was, you all saw me dancing!" said Monkey.

"I was dancing too," said Elephant.

"Me too," said Lizard.

"And me," said Snake.

"Somebody wasn't," accused Lion. "Who was it?"

Leopard stepped forward. Everyone looked at him, waiting in hushed silence. He opened his mouth to speak up. "There's no way to settle this. What's done is done," he said. "Let's just put it behind us and carry on dancing." He looked up hopefully at Lion, wondering if he could throw everyone off the scent before someone suspected him.

"There *is* a way to settle this," growled Lion. "Somebody is lying and I'm going to find out who."

Leopard shrank back in fear. He knew he should admit what he had done, but instead he just hoped Lion would let it go.

"Right," continued Lion in his "I'm in charge" voice. "We can all take part in a test to see who is lying."

Most of the animals nodded enthusiastically, but

Antelope looked confused. “How can we tell who has eaten our yams when they are already gone?” she asked.

Lion cleared his throat to make sure they all could hear him and replied, “We can do the test of fire.” He smiled triumphantly, for this was a well-known test among the animals. Lion reminded them about how it would work. “We will make a small fire in a hole in the ground. This will be our firepit and everyone will take turns to jump over it. Whoever is telling the truth will land safely on the other side. Whoever is lying will be so full of shame and yams that they will fall into the pit.”

They all agreed to this test, except for Snake, who slid up to the feet of Lion, stretched his long neck up high to face him and said, “What about you, Lion? How do we know that you are not the yam thief? You must jump the pit as well,” he hissed.

Lion did not like being challenged, but he agreed to also jump over the fire.

They all lined up behind each other to take their turn. Hippopotamus went first.

Hippo is so big and heavy, he might fall in the pit anyway, Leopard hoped. Hippopotamus took a deep breath and trotted over to the firepit, letting his stubby legs fly through the air. He landed heavily on the other side and everyone cheered. Next it was the turn of the zebras. They shook their manes to limber up and galloped at top speed towards the fire. Their eyes were fixed firmly on the other side as each one jumped over the flickering flames. Their legs stretched out like leaping ballerinas and everyone admired how graceful they looked. The monkeys lined up next, giggling and singing loudly as they each took their turn. They knew they had nothing to fear. One by one they sprang up high in the air with their tails curling behind them. When it was Lion's turn, he took his time, strolling proudly up to the pit. Because this test was his idea, he wanted to show off his jumping skills. He stopped right before the fire, leaned backwards on to his legs and then catapulted himself over the flames. He landed on all fours as if he was used to doing this every day.

All the animals flew swiftly over the flickering flames until it came to Snake. He slowly crawled up the trunk of a tree which hung just above the firepit. Everyone wondered where he was going. Snake slithered along a branch and then pushed himself forward off the tree. His body bounced over the fire like a coiled spring until he landed head first with a THUMP on the other side.

Leopard was the last to jump. He could feel all the yams heavy in his tummy. He nervously began to sing, hoping to pluck up enough courage to jump. He finished a chorus and then sang again. Everyone started to wonder why he was taking so long. Why wouldn't he jump over the flames?

"Jump, Leopard, jump," they all sang in chorus. "Jump, Leopard, jump."

Leopard's stomach felt heavier and heavier from all of the yams he had eaten. He stared at the flames of the fire, then finally ran as fast as he could, trying to lift his body into the air in a big jump. His legs stretched out over the flames, but his tummy was too full and he landed straight in the fire, falling on to the hot coals. He jumped out quickly and rolled around on the grass.

But it was too late.

His fur had been burned off in patches and now he had dark spots all over his body.

"You are the thief!" shouted Lion. The warthogs raised their tusks in anger, squealing loudly. "How could you do this, Leopard?" they cried out in disappointment.

From the treetops you could hear a cacophony of noise rise up from all the animals who were outraged at Leopard.

Jackal HOWLED.

Hyena SCREAMED.

Elephant HOOTED.

Snake HISSED.

Baboon BARKED.

Leopard hung his head low and stared at the ground. "I'm very sorry for eating all of the yams. I couldn't help myself," he said.

"You did help yourself!" cried Hippopotamus. But he was secretly pleased that someone else was more greedy than him.

Leopard felt very ashamed at what he had done. "I'm sorry I didn't tell you that it was me. I knew you would be angry and didn't want to be punished," he said, with his eyes still facing down.

"Yes, we are angry, but it is better to be punished for telling the truth than to be rewarded for lies," replied Lion sagely. "Now all that remains is to decide what your punishment should be." Lion and the other animals turned away from Leopard and began to discuss Leopard's fate in hushed tones. A few of the animals suggested that he should be banished from their land and never allowed to return again. He had stolen their feast and lied, after all. But Lion took pity on Leopard, who had faced all of their wrath.

"No," decided Lion. "Leopard has been punished enough. I think he has learned his lesson. Don't you all agree?" he asked all of the animals. Their faces softened and they nodded in agreement that Leopard had indeed been punished enough. Lion turned back to Leopard and proclaimed, "We will not punish you further. Your brown fur is now marked with spots for ever and will remain with you and your descendants as a sign of your guilt."

That is why Leopard can no longer blend into the forest. To this very day he still has spots on his fur as a reminder of his greedy behaviour.

Aunt Misery's Starfruit Tree

(PUERTO RICO)

This is a traditional folktale from Puerto Rico which explains why we have misery in the world. It is a story about a clever old woman who uses her wits to defeat Death . . .

On a small island in the Caribbean Sea, there once lived an old woman. Her most prized possession was a beautiful starfruit tree that grew the sweetest fruit.

Each day, the boys and girls in the village would sneak up to her wooden house, which sat high upon its wooden stilts, and climb into her tree. Swinging and laughing, they plucked the delicious fruit which hung from each branch like yellow, star-shaped diamonds.

"You little thieves. Get down from my tree!" the old woman would scold, but they just laughed and called her "Aunt Misery", running away from her with the sweet fruit from her tree. It happened so often that the name "Aunt Misery" stuck with everyone in the village and they forgot her real name.

One day, the rain beat down hard like a drum and the sea breeze carried a new visitor through the village. He made his way past the market stalls that sold fresh fish, through the mango groves and cocoa fields, until he finally reached Aunt Misery's house. He knocked on her door and explained that he was a poor traveller in need of help.

"Can you spare some food and a bed for the

night?" he asked. His young face was kind and his voice was soothing.

Aunt Misery rarely welcomed visitors but decided that as he had asked so politely, she would make an exception. She made a simple yet hearty meal of peas and rice flavoured with herbs and spices which the hungry traveller devoured quickly. After eating, the two of them sat outside on Aunt Misery's veranda, sipping bittersweet juice from the fruit of a mauby tree, listening to the chorus of crickets and tree frogs.

"I would like to repay you for your hospitality," said the young man. "I can't offer much, but I can grant you one wish, anything you want."

The old woman's eyes shone in the darkness at the stranger's words. She knew he must be a sorcerer in disguise. She thought hard and then said, "I wish for anyone who climbs my starfruit tree to remain stuck in its branches until I release them." She couldn't wait to teach the local children a lesson for stealing her beloved starfruit.

The following morning, just as dawn kissed the sky, the young man packed up his few belongings and tapped the bark of the old woman's starfruit tree. He granted her wish and carried on with his journey.

Later that day, three boys came, eager to pluck starfruit from the tree. They climbed up high and swung on the gnarled branches, filling their school bags with the long-fingered fruit.

When Aunt Misery stepped out from her house, they jeered and sang:

Ol' Aunt Misery come for we
She can't catch us
Up high in the tree.

But when they tried to get down, they found their feet would not move. No matter how hard they pushed, they could not climb down from the starfruit tree.

They were stuck.

"Ha!" cried Aunt Misery. "And there you will stay until I decide otherwise."

The boys were terrified and begged her to let them come down.

Finally, just before night came and the fireflies lit up the grass, Aunt Misery declared: "I will release you if you promise never to steal from my starfruit tree again."

The boys agreed and scrambled away, yelling

as they ran, "Aunt Misery is a witch! She's an ol' witch!" When the villagers heard what she had done to the boys, some of them weren't surprised. "I knew she was an ol' witch," a few of them said, and they warned their children not to bother her again.

Time passed, as time does. Both Aunt Misery and her tree grew crooked and lined with age, but the tree's golden starfruit continued to bring her happiness.

One cool evening, the sea breeze swirled and snaked its way through the village again. This time it brought a different visitor to Aunt Misery's door. His dark eyes were hollow and his voice carried no warmth.

"I am Death," he said slowly. "I have come to take you with me."

Aunt Misery knew that it was her time, but she was not ready to die. She thought of her golden starfruit, wanting to taste it one more time, and suddenly she had an idea.

"Before you take me, Death, will you please climb up my tree and pick a starfruit for me? I am too old to climb and I would like to have one last taste of my delicious fruit," she explained.

Death nodded solemnly and climbed the tree. He reached with his long limbs and picked some of the fruit, whilst Aunt Misery looked on from below. When he finished picking, he tried to place his feet on the lower branches, but they bounced back up again. *What is wrong with my feet?* he thought to himself, thinking that perhaps the branches were too far away. He moved around the tree to the other side, but the same thing happened. He climbed a little higher to see if he could still go up and then quickly realized that he could not get back down.

"What spell have you cast?" he called down to Aunt Misery, noticing that she was laughing out loud.

"Oh, just a little something that only I can change," she squealed with delight. Death was stuck in Aunt Misery's starfruit tree and there was nothing he could do about it.

"I have work to do," complained Death. "Release me at once or you'll be sorry!" he threatened. But Aunt Misery ignored him. She was so happy her plan had worked that she did a little dance. As long as Death could not take her, she could live for ever and continue to enjoy her starfruit every day. She went back inside her house and slept soundly that night.

The following morning a boy named Edmond came to test out Aunt Misery's starfruit tree. He did not believe the story his friends told. As he approached Aunt Misery's house, he saw Death sitting comfortably at the top of the tree.

"Who are you?" Edmund asked as he walked around the tree.

"I am Death," he said gloomily.

Edmund thought for a minute, wondering why Death would be in Aunt Misery's tree.

"Why are you sitting in the tree?

"Aunt Misery trapped me."

"Are you stuck?" Edmund asked.

"Yes," sighed Death. He felt quite embarrassed to be found in the tree.

Edmund started laughing and pointing at Death, singing,

Death is stuck in Aunt Misery's tree.
With all his power, he can't get free.
He can't get up and he can't get down,
His face is long, like his big black gown.

He ran back to the village to tell everyone that Death was trapped in Aunt Misery's tree and couldn't get down.

Meanwhile, she was content in her little wooden house. She was happy spending her days cooking delicious stews, making sweet drinks and tending to her animals.

But Death being unable to leave meant that no one in the village could die. The village became overcrowded, as the young people grew up and the old people still remained. The funeral parlour was empty and the gravediggers had nothing to do. Everyone became lazy, as they knew they would live for ever. Jobs were left unfinished and parks were overflowing with people sitting around, bored and doing nothing. Queues at the shops snaked all around the village, with people hoping to get things to eat. There wasn't enough food growing fast enough to feed so many people. The hospital remained empty as no one became sick, but people grew old and tired of living.

One evening, just before the crickets and bull-frogs began their chorus of croaking, a few of the older villagers gathered together to find a solution. They sat under the flame trees in the market square and listened to each other's ideas.

Dr Rummy spoke first. He was bored now that nobody was visiting his surgery. "One of us needs to go and speak to Aunt Misery. Explain to her what is happening in the village because of the way she has trapped Death."

"Maybe she doesn't realize," offered Maria, who ran the local bakery. Her business was booming now that no one was worried about eating too much. She was overwhelmed with requests for sweet bread rolls, guava pastries and delicious papaya cakes.

"Maybe she doesn't care," said Mateo, whose pharmacy was always empty because no one needed to buy medicines now that they could not die. "She is happy and not affected by anything going on in the village," he reminded them.

"But what if Death finds a way to escape?" said another. "He will come to take her like everyone else. She will never agree to let him go if he will take her with him."

It was agreed that they would visit Aunt Misery and beg her to release Death, so that life could go on without all of these worries.

Early the next morning a few of the villagers headed over to Aunt Misery's home. They saw

Death sitting in the starfruit tree and wondered if he had a plan for getting down.

"Death, how long are you going to stay up there?" they asked.

Death shrugged. "Ask Aunt Misery," he said, pointing as she came towards them. Aunt Misery had heard voices and was surprised to see visitors.

"What are you all doing here?" she asked crossly. After all, they had never visited her before.

The villagers looked humble and said, "Aunt Misery, we know you don't want Death to take you, but the village is overcrowded. Us old people are getting older, the sick can't die and there's not enough food to feed everyone."

Aunt Misery's heart softened. She had not realized that other people might still need Death around. For her, he was an unwanted visitor.

"Well, I can't release him," she said stubbornly. "He'll take me with him and I'm not going!"

"You're such an ol' MISERY," cried one of the villagers. "We need Death to get back to his job."

Aunt Misery's face turned sour and she shooed them off her land. After feeding her animals and tending to her plants, she sat stewing for a while, thinking over what had been said. Despite her anger at being called an ol' misery, she didn't want to cause anyone any harm and wondered if there was a way to make everyone happy, including Death.

Later that evening, she made a suggestion. "If you never come back for me," she said to Death, "I will release you from the starfruit tree."

Death loved to make a bargain but did not want to let her off that easily. She had kept him from his work, which he enjoyed.

"I will leave you for a few more years if you release me," he said, hoping that she would agree.

"No," said Aunt Misery, and turned to walk away.

Death did not like being in this position. Aunt Misery was completely in charge.

"I could punish you right now and turn you to stone." Death's eyes blazed angrily. But Aunt Misery was too clever and not scared of his threats.

"Well, you'd still be stuck in my tree," she sniped back. With a sigh Death relented, knowing he had no other options. Ol' Misery's deal was the only one he was going to get, and so he agreed to let her live for ever if she released him. The pair shook hands, and Death went about his business. He had actually quite liked his break from taking lives but was happy to get back to work.

So that is why we still have misery in our world today. Aunt Misery made a deal with Death, and she is still alive somewhere, as miserable as ever . . .

Spirits And Shape-Shifters

These stories feature ghosts, animals and people who have the power to transform into enchanted creatures. Watch out, they may leap out from the page and draw you in . . .

Soliday and the Bird of Darkness

(JAMAICA)

In this story, a young hero called Soliday tries to save his people's kingdom from a monstrous bird whose black wings block out the sun, forcing the world into darkness.

Far away on an island filled with mountains of fresh spices and cocoa trees, there once lived a queen. Her palace of white stone walls and pillars sat high on the greenest hill. Every morning she opened her window shutters and stared out at the bright blue Caribbean Sea. From her balcony, she watched the sun rise. It was her favourite time of day, smelling the salty sea breeze and feeling sunshine across her face.

One morning, she awoke as usual and was alarmed to see that it was still dark outside. There was no sunlight sprinkling through her shutters and no sound from the birds singing their early morning songs. She checked her clock on the wall. The long hand was at twelve and the short hand at six. She listened for the gentle *tick, tick, tick* but instead she heard shrieking from her maid, running along the corridor.

"The world is ending! The world is ending!" She came rushing into the queen's bedroom, waving her arms wildly in the air. "My queen, the sun has not risen in the sky."

The queen hastily dressed, feeling anxious about what she might find. She hurried to her advisors, who were on their way with worrying news.

"My queen, our island has been visited by the giant bird. His wings are so wide, they completely block out our sun," said one gravely.

"Where is this bird of darkness? Why is it here?" she asked, hardly believing the news herself.

They told her that the bird was called *Mancrow*. Half man, half crow, he had long black wings and sharp golden talons. His body and wings were so huge that the sunlight was hidden from the island. But as to why he was in their kingdom, no one knew.

Mancrow was perched on the highest branch of the tallest tree in one of their forests. He sat there devouring their fruits from nearby trees. Knowing that she had to do something, the queen sent soldiers with bows and arrows to rid them of the bird of darkness. After several days, they returned shamefaced and empty-handed.

"Our arrows could not reach, he was sitting too high," one soldier said. "We even tried throwing rocks but nothing got near him," another explained.

"What are we going to do?" she asked them, pacing up and down. Her advisors shrugged and scratched their heads. No one had any ideas of how to get rid of the giant bird.

With the sun unable to shine on the island, people's days were filled with dark, grey nights. They slept in darkness and woke up to darkness. Children went to school in darkness and played outside in darkness. No one travelled from the coast into the mountains, for fear of losing their way. No one travelled from the mountains to the coast, in case they fell over the edge of a cliff. Grass could not grow, flowers could not bloom, leaves turned yellow and died. Meanwhile, in a forest filled with sweet fruits, Mancrow stretched his long black neck and sucked the juice from ripe mangoes and tamarind pods. He cracked open heart-shaped soursops and swallowed the creamy fruit inside.

One dark evening, the queen stood outside on her balcony. She listened for the familiar sound of the crickets chirping but heard nothing. Instead of seeing bright fireflies dancing between the trees, she saw a wall of blackness. Then she noticed a small crowd of people waiting outside of her palace gates. There were mothers and fathers carrying babies, children looking tired and scared, old people with walking sticks, and others leaning against the palm trees.

"They have come to ask you to get rid of the bird of darkness," said one of her guards. "They will not leave the palace grounds until something is done."

The queen paced up and down in her throne room and summoned her advisors.

"It has been nearly a month since that wretched bird plunged our island into darkness. We must find a way to kill it!" she raged, becoming more frustrated at their blank faces.

"Send more soldiers," suggested one advisor.

"No," said the queen. "That does nothing. Their arrows don't even reach the bird. There is nothing for it. If you have no better ideas, I will have to ask all our people to help," she decided.

The advisors dismissed her idea immediately. "If our trained soldiers cannot defeat Mancrow, what will a farmer or fisherman do?" they said, almost laughing in her face. But the queen ignored them and stood on her balcony to speak to the crowd of people below.

"Listen, everyone. I will offer a reward to the person who can rid us of this Mancrow. I pledge half of my wealth and riches shall be given to whoever can kill the bird and let our sunlight return."

The crowd murmured down below, wondering

who among them would be brave enough to face the giant bird of darkness.

Word soon spread across the island about the queen's generous reward. Day after day, people set off into the forest, hoping to find and kill Mancrow. Some of them arrived at the foot of the tree where he sat and were so terrified at the sight of his hollow black eyes in the middle of his dark, feathery face that they ran straight back home. Others ignored their fears and aimed their arrows at his man-shaped body, but he was far too high in the trees for them to reach.

One young man named Soliday lived with his grandmother in a small house on the edge of the island. They had very little money and the food they grew was running low. She was a seamstress, who made colourful *quadrille* dresses for dancers on the island. Without any sunlight, her eyes were failing, making it hard to see her needle and thread.

"Oh, look at this *bandana* skirt! My stitches have gone wonky and uneven." She held up the bright red skirt. "Mrs Clarke will not pay for mistakes like this," she complained, squinting her eyes under the candlelight. Soliday thought his grandmother worked too hard. He wished that he could help more. Now that the island was cloaked in darkness, his work in the fields had vanished, which meant that he had no money to buy food. He turned to his grandmother and said, "Tomorrow I am going to use the last of our money to buy arrows."

"Why do you need to buy arrows, Soliday? Are you going to hunt in the darkness?" she asked, thinking they needed food instead of arrows.

"I am going to hunt, but not for food. I will buy arrows to defeat Mancrow and win the queen's reward. I must try and bring sunlight back to our island again."

His grandmother thought he was foolish to think he could defeat Mancrow, but nevertheless gave him her last two coins and a spiced fruit bun for his journey. Whilst he was in town, Soliday bumped into his neighbour, a long-legged man named Jackroy, who was leaning against a wall, watching people go by.

"Hello there, Soliday. What brings you to town?" asked Jackroy.

"Greetings, Jackroy." Soliday nodded and tried to hurry on his way. He did not trust Jackroy, who had a reputation for tricking people out of their belongings. But Jackroy looked Soliday up and down and noticed his travelling bag with the bow and six arrows. "Why do you need all those arrows?" he asked suspiciously. But Soliday refused to explain, rushing past him quickly.

Once he had left Jackroy behind, Soliday made his way across the cocoa fields that lay almost bare. He knew that Mancrow was somewhere on Blue Mountain Peak, so he walked deep into the forest of slowly dying trees, heading for the mountain. He trudged through the layers of leaves that now carpeted the ground, carrying a small lamp to light his way. He didn't hear the soft sound of footsteps behind him, or notice that Jackroy was following him.

In the darkness, Soliday braved the narrow lanes which twisted and turned higher and higher up the mountainside. He rested beside tumbling waterfalls and walked through blue mist hovering in the air. But he wasn't alone. Little did he know, but behind him, steady and sure, Jackroy kept up with Soliday's swift pace, hiding behind trees and making sure that Soliday didn't notice him. He was suspicious of Soliday and had decided to follow him, thinking that he could keep him close and discover what he was up to.

For three dark days and three dark nights, Soliday climbed and searched for the tree which held Mancrow. On the fourth day, near the top of Blue Mountain Peak, Soliday came to the foot of the flamboyant tree. Its bright red flowers spread out above him, like a scarlet umbrella. The enormous bird of darkness was sleeping in the branches. He opened one beady eye when he heard Soliday approaching. Soliday aimed his arrow at Mancrow's wing and sang out.

Mancrow, Mancrow, today you will die.
You have taken our crops and darkened our sky.

The giant bird of darkness opened his long beak, revealing a golden tongue, and replied.

Soliday, Soliday, you are far from home.
Put down your arrow and leave me alone.

Soliday didn't reply, instead releasing an arrow which shot up high into the tree and struck the tip of Mancrow's wing. Two black feathers fell off and floated downward to the ground beside Soliday. Mancrow slipped down to the next branch below.

Soliday aimed another arrow at Mancrow and sang out again.

Mancrow, Mancrow, today you will die.
You have taken our crops and darkened our sky.

The giant bird of darkness tightened his golden talons on the tree branch and replied.

Soliday, Soliday, you are far from home.
Put down your arrow and leave me alone.

Soliday released his second arrow, which shot up high into the tree and struck the edge of Mancrow's leg. Two more black feathers fell off and floated downward to the ground beside Soliday. Mancrow slipped down to the next branch below. Soliday aimed another arrow at Mancrow and sang out again.

Mancrow, Mancrow, today you will die.
You have taken our crops and darkened our sky.

The giant bird of darkness spread out his long wings and replied.

Soliday, Soliday, you are far from home.
Put down your arrow and leave me alone.

Soliday released his third arrow, which shot up high into the tree and struck Mancrow's neck. Another pair of black feathers fell off and floated downward to the ground beside Soliday. Mancrow slipped down to the next branch below. Soliday had three more arrows left. He aimed each one at the giant bird which had brought darkness to his people. Each time he sang out and wounded Mancrow. Each time Mancrow replied and slipped down to the lowest branch before finally falling on to the ground, dead. At last blinding sunshine appeared across the sky, bringing daylight back to the island. Soliday rejoiced by dancing around on the spot, singing, "He's down, he's down, I brought Mancrow down!"

All along, Jackroy had been lurking behind a breadfruit tree, spying on Soliday as he shot down Mancrow. Now that Mancrow was dead, he crouched down behind the rocks and waited until Soliday was walking steadily down the twisting path. Jackroy quietly followed behind, and when he was close enough, he reached out with his long arms and pushed Soliday over the edge of the mountainside. Soliday went tumbling down the rocky path below.

"That's the end of you," laughed Jackroy, and rushed on to the queen's palace to claim the reward for killing the giant Mancrow.

"I am the one who shot the enormous bird of darkness out of the flamboyant tree with my six arrows," Jackroy boasted to the queen and her guards. She was overjoyed at the return of their sunlight. She praised Jackroy for his bravery and skill, never once suspecting that he could be lying.

"Now for your reward," announced the queen, who was overjoyed to have sunshine surrounding her kingdom. She signalled to one of her guards to bring out treasures from her chamber. Jackroy's eyes widened as they brought out trays filled with gold coins and jars of precious stones. He rubbed his hands with eagerness at the thought of all the things he could buy with his new wealth. But just as the queen was about to hand them over, a loud commotion could be heard in the palace grounds. The guards entered with Soliday, whose hair was dishevelled and clothes were soaking wet, but otherwise unharmed. After Jackroy had pushed him over the rocky edge, he had fallen down into a pool of natural spring water. It flowed down the mountainside, taking Soliday safely with it. With the sun now dazzling from the sky, lighting up his path, he was able to find his way back to the queen's palace easily.

Now the two men, Soliday and Jackroy, stood before the queen, each insisting that they were telling the truth.

"Jackroy is a liar," cried Soliday. "I am the one who killed Mancrow and brought back sunlight to the island."

"Soliday is a liar," cried Jackroy. "I am the one who killed Mancrow and brought back sunlight to the island."

The queen did not know who to believe. She looked from one to the other in confusion. Luckily, Soliday knew just what to do. He reached into his bag and brought out Mancrow's golden talons.

"I cut these from Mancrow's legs after I shot him down from the tree. This is proof that I alone have killed him and deserve this reward. Jackroy is the liar, not me." Horrified that she had almost given her treasure to the wrong person, the queen demanded Jackroy be banished immediately, never allowed to return to their kingdom. Looking shamefaced, Jackroy was dragged away by the queen's guards and Soliday given his rightful reward of treasures from her chamber. His grandmother squealed with delight when she heard the news. Their lives were now changed for ever because of Soliday's bravery. Never again would she need to spend her days and nights sewing or worrying about money.

The entire island was jubilant that the bird of darkness had been defeated and that sunlight had returned. They rejoiced and feasted for days. Soliday and his grandmother were honoured guests at the palace, dining with the queen on ackee and saltfish, curried goat and sweet potato pudding. They ate and danced in celebration with the rest of the island folk until the golden sun went down and rose again.

The Golden Comb of Mama D'Leau

(Haiti)

Stories about Mama D'Leau are told all over the Caribbean islands. Sometimes she is referred to as "Water Mama" or "Mama D'Low". Half woman, half sea snake, Mama D'leau is known as the protector and healer of river animals. In this version of the story, a young fisherman tries to steal Mama D'Leau's magical golden comb and is tormented by her as a punishment.

Early every morning on the island of Haiti, fishermen set sail across the deep blue Caribbean Sea. Before the sun rises in the sky, they cast their nets into the water. By mid-morning, huge hauls of salt-water fish are dragged onto their small boats and taken to the markets for selling each day.

A fisherman called Pierre was the youngest of three brothers who lived in the north of the island near the Port-de-Paix. The three boys each had their own small fishing boats and set sail most mornings from the bay, where the shoreline curved like a golden crescent. Pierre and his brothers loved to sail out to where the crystal-blue waters were deepest. Green sea turtles, flamingo snails and clinging crabs could be seen swimming alongside colourful fishes. The brothers cast their nets for their daily catch of fish before returning to shore. But Pierre's net always remained empty, without any fish. No matter how hard he tried or how long he waited, the fish were never tempted by his bait and avoided his net. Poor Pierre returned to shore every day without any fish, and his brothers never failed to tease him mercilessly.

"Look at Pierre's net. It's more empty than his head!" they laughed, dragging their nets filled with tilapia and long-clawed lobsters. “Stay home and bake bread, you’re no fisherman!” they said, and left him to hang his head in shame all the way home, wishing he wasn’t such a failure. How he longed to make them all proud and see him as a fisherman too.

One afternoon whilst sitting in the middle of the sea with the sun blazing down upon their heads, Pierre dragged in his empty net from the water and sighed. He knew that unlike his brothers, he had caught nothing that day. He packed up his bait and decided to leave his brothers to their fishing in the sea. He sailed his small boat back towards the bay, but instead of heading to shore, he drifted along in the direction of the Trois Rivières. It was the widest river that ran through the island with dense forest on either side. The largest variety of fish could be found in this river, but fishermen never cast their nets here. They were afraid of being punished by the fierce sea creature Mama D’Leau. Pierre had grown up hearing fishermen describe her as half woman and half sea snake; from the waist down her female shape was said to take on the form of a coiling serpent’s tail, which she used to lash anyone harming the water creatures.

Pierre's grandfather told him many times, "Never fish in the river, Pierre. You will regret it if you do." He always finished by reminding Pierre about the night he met Mama D'Leau.

"Seeing her was so terrifying that my hair turned crystal white overnight," he exclaimed, opening his eyes so wide, Pierre felt he would drown in them. He confessed to Pierre how he and his friends were caught by Mama D'Leau that night, tipping rubbish into the ocean. She had risen from the depths of the sea and whipped up a tempestuous storm, which sent Pierre's grandfather and his friends hurtling over the crashing waves. She hissed at them with her venomous tail and screamed out a warning which he never forgot:

Fishermen of the island, I catch you fouling
the sea.
All of these waters are protected by me.
If you dare to harm creatures near my sea bed
I gon' lash you for eternity and
You'll wish you were dead.

After receiving such a terrible threat, none of the local fishermen would ever dare to pollute the waters or go fishing in the river. But Pierre was feeling so bitter about being teased by his brothers for never catching any fish that he no longer cared about the stories he'd heard growing up. He wasn't even sure he believed his grandfather's tall tale about Mama D'Leau. *Those stories are made up just to stop us fishing in the river. I don't believe she really exists*, he thought to himself. Gliding his boat out to the middle of the river as it snaked away from his town, Pierre cast his fishing net into a protected part of the water where it was illegal to fish. He recalled his grandfather's words: "Never fish in the river, Pierre." But Pierre was desperate to prove to his brothers that he could bring home some fish. *They think I can't catch any fish, but I'll surely have more luck in this river than the sea*, he decided, and waited quietly in his boat, hoping that no one would see him.

It was that sleepy time of the day when no one was around. People were taking an afternoon nap or sheltering from the scorching sunshine, so the river was deserted. Pierre sat patiently under the glare of the sun and the watchful eyes of the freshwater birds poking around in the mud. Suddenly, the fishing net started to pull from his hands. He struggled to hold it and realized that it was feeling very heavy, almost too heavy for his small body to lift. He jumped up to steady himself, holding on tightly. The net tugged again, nearly dragging him overboard. Loud swishing and whooshing sounds were coming from below, sounding like rattlesnakes. It was a strange sensation and he wondered what it could be. Pierre held on fast and peered down into the murky water excitedly. Orange-and-green eyes peered back at him. Spiky fins flipped and flapped, poking through the holes of his net. Long red claws stretched out towards him, snipping and snapping near his nose. He grinned eagerly as swarms of fishes, lobsters and crabs filled his net for the first time. They swirled around in a giant ball, lashing each other with their tails. Moving as fast as he could, he dragged his net into the boat and stared in wonder at the sight of his catch. Conch, crabs and crayfish darted around in the net, which was filled to the brim. This was his first catch and he was overjoyed.

"Wait until my brothers see all of this fish I've caught! They won't be able to laugh at me now." Pierre clapped his hands, grinning with delight as he imagined the look on his brothers' faces when he showed them his catch. Settling back down in his seat, he prepared to sail back home when he saw something gold shining out from the wriggling mass of fish. *What could that be?* he thought, and reached inside the net to pull it out. There in his hands, he held a small golden comb. The handle was inlaid with glittering gems whose colours could match any rainbow. He ran his fingers over the golden edge of the comb and felt the intricately carved flowers along the back. He wondered who could own such a precious item. Pierre tucked the comb into his shirt pocket and glanced around to see if anyone was watching. "Grandfather was wrong. The river *is* the place for me to fish," he seethed to himself. Satisfied that no one had seen him take fish from the river, he sailed back home to show off his first catch of fish.

"What a catch of the best fish you have," said one brother to Pierre. "I never thought you could do it," exclaimed the other, slapping Pierre on his back as a sign of approval. "I'm really proud of you, my son," said their mother, relieved that he had found his way at last. That evening, the whole family feasted on some of the fish from Pierre's catch. They made conch fritters and roasted tilapia with bell peppers.

Everyone praised Pierre and congratulated him on his fishing success.

Later that night, when he was alone in his room, Pierre took the golden comb from his pocket and pulled it through his hair. The teeth of the comb slid through his tight black curls and whispered a soft melody in his ears. As he listened carefully, he realized the comb was revealing the secrets of the sea with each stroke through his hair. Murmurs of buried treasure, the best places to find fish and the most peaceful waters were whispered in his ears. Pierre was ecstatic! No longer would he have to suffer his brothers' taunts. They would have to accept him as one of the best fishermen on the island. He hid the comb under his pillow, thinking that no one knew of his secret.

But someone *did* know. A long way down below the surface of the river, a furious Mama D'Leau raged in her underwater kingdom. She sat on her throne of shimmering coral and seagrass, furious that someone had fished in the river and taken her magical golden comb. She called out to her helpers, the fairymaids. These creatures were half women, half fish, and they followed her every command.

"Come quickly, my fairymaids, I have a task for

you all!" Her voice echoed along the sandy riverbed, inside the waterfall caves where the fairymaids lurked. These graceful creatures, with long flowing hair and giant fish tails, raced through the waters at great speed after they heard the call from Mama D'Leau. They found her fuming in her palace of stony white coral.

"We heard you calling, Mama D'Leau. Tell us what you need." The fairymaids circled around her throne, waiting to hear her command.

"I've let my golden comb, my precious treasure which knows all the secrets of the sea, slip through my fingers, and that wretched boy has fished in our river and found it. Use your powers to bring it back to me. Visit him in his dreams. Entice him with buried riches. Bewitch him with the promise of your love, and if that does not work, I will curse the entire village until he returns what belongs to me." Mama D'Leau's eyes flashed with sparks of lightning and her long strands of hair weaved around her head, transforming into slithering, hissing snakes. The fairymaids smiled at each other, for they loved having a reason to trick anyone who lived on land.

That night, one of Mama D'Leau's fairymaids visited Pierre in his dreams. She was sitting on a rock by a lagoon of aqua-blue water. In the dream, her face was mostly hidden by dark wavy hair. She had the upper body of a girl but from the waist down, her body curved into the shape of a fish's tail with iridescent scales. She sang a sad, mournful song asking Pierre to bring the golden comb to her by the lagoon.

He awoke from the dream feeling as though it had been real. He could still see the magical creature when he closed his eyes, and the memory of her words echoed in his ears. She had asked him to visit the lagoon to return the comb to her in exchange for treasure. Pierre could think of nothing but obeying her wishes. He felt under his pillow and was relieved to feel the comb still there safely. But as soon as he held the golden comb, his desire to keep it close to him was too strong to fight. The colours from the gems glistened in his hands. He ran his fingers over the golden edges and thought, *Now you belong to me. This is all the treasure I need.* He decided to see if the comb would whisper secrets again. He combed his hair with it and listened to the gentle words singing in his ears. The comb told him to sail out near to Île de la Tortue, an island shaped like a tortoiseshell. There he was to dive into the sea, where he would find abandoned riches.

Pierre made his way out to sea that morning, ahead of his brothers. Clutching the golden comb to his chest, he felt a new surge of confidence for the first time in his life. Any doubts he felt about his fishing skills melted away into the salty sea. He was proud to be on a new adventure, all by himself.

Before the sun had peeped across the horizon, he reached Île de la Tortue. The contours of the rocky island came into view as the morning mist cleared. He cast his net into the wine-dark sea, just as the golden comb had told him to do. Within moments the net filled up with swarming, wriggling fish. "I knew it!" cried Pierre as he struggled to haul in his net. "The golden comb has brought me good luck." Just as he prepared to dive down and search for treasure, a figure on the rocks caught his eye. A young woman was sitting very still on the edge of the mountainous island. Pierre moved his boat closer to try to get a better look. She had long, dark, wavy hair covering the top half of her body. Her legs were a giant fish's tail with two small fins at the end which flapped gently on the rocks. Pierre nearly fell out of his boat in shock. *She looks just like the magical creature from my dream. She is real. She really exists*, he thought with amazement. He quickly gathered his wits and called out to her. "Who are you?" he said. "What is your name?" The fairymaid dived into the sea and surfaced near his boat, with only her head and shoulders just above the water. She stared blankly at Pierre. Her hollow eyes were as dark as coffee beans. She beckoned him into the water.

"Do you want me to follow you?" he asked hesitantly. He felt strangely drawn to her serene face but suspected she may want to take the golden comb from him. He reached into his pocket and pulled out the comb. Holding it out in front of him, he said, "Is this what you are looking for? Is this what you want?"

The fairymaid's face quickly changed, her soft smile contorted into a hideous snarl, revealing tiny, spiky rows of sharp teeth. She hissed loudly and in one swift move she flipped up beside the boat and tried to grab the comb from Pierre's hand. He was too fast and leaned back, shoving it quickly into his pocket. Pierre picked up the oars of his boat and rowed as fast as he could back to his side of the island. His heart was thumping loudly in his ears and his hands burned as he pushed and pulled with all his might. He was terrified that the fairymaid would jump at him again, but when he looked back, he saw no sign of her.

At home, Pierre's brothers were once again amazed at his fishing skills and wondered how his fortunes had suddenly changed. Pierre revelled in their praise, but he kept the secret of the golden comb to himself. After all his brothers' teasing, he did not want to share his secrets with them.

Day after day, Pierre cast his net at sea wherever the golden comb sent him. He captured bountiful amounts of fish, which he was able to give to his family and sell to market traders. Sometimes he dived deep below and found piles of golden coins which he stored away secretly in his room. But although Pierre's fortunes had turned around, he wasn't happy. Instead, he was worn out and wretched, drowning in misery each night. As soon as he closed his eyes, fairymaids visited him with dreams, clouding his mind with mournful songs and promises of riches, pleading for him to return Mama D'Leau's magical golden comb.

Before long, his mother became worried about his appearance and spoke to his brothers.

"Is anything wrong with Pierre? Ever since he started catching fish, he looks haggard and worn out," she said, hoping that Pierre had confided in his brothers.

"Oh, Mama, don't worry. He's just a weakling," they laughed.

"He's not used to the life of a fisherman yet," they said, trying to convince their mother that perhaps Pierre was simply not as strong as them. But she didn't believe them and decided to investigate for herself. That evening, she waited until her boys were out for a walk and searched Pierre's room. Desperately, she tumbled through drawers, checked under his bed and peeped inside bags, but found nothing. Just as she was about to give up, a shiny object caught her eye on the floor in the corner of the room. It was a single gold coin. *Where could he have found this?* she wondered, knowing they were not wealthy enough to own gold coins. She moved a small cupboard and a bag of gold coins came tumbling out. In the middle of the pile of shimmering riches lay Mama D'Leau's golden comb. She gasped with disbelief, not knowing what to think, just as Pierre appeared in the doorway.

"Mother, I can explain," he said hurriedly,

snatching the comb away. His eyes were wild and his hands moved frantically across the floor, gathering up all the gold coins. At that moment she did not recognize her son and knew that he must be in trouble. She grabbed his arm and demanded that he tell her everything.

Pierre hung his head low and said, "I'm sorry, Mother. I fished in the river and found this golden comb. It led me to this treasure and where to find fish. A fairymaid even tried to take it back from me. I know I shouldn't have kept it but I can't resist its magic. When I have the comb, I feel invincible, as if I can do anything!" His voice hardened as he thought about the comb and how it helped him beat his brothers at fishing. She looked into his eyes, hoping to find a trace of remorse. But his eyes were dark, like obsidian rock. Everything finally made sense to her. Pierre's strange behaviour, his new success at fishing. She knew the stories of Mama D'leau and was horrified that her son did not believe them.

"Your dreams of torment will continue until you return that comb to the river," said his mother sternly, leaving him with this advice: "At the water's edge, call out to the fairymaid and ask her to release you from her spell. When she arrives, leave the comb on the ground and walk away without looking back."

Pierre nodded in agreement, but he had no intention of returning the comb. *The comb belongs to me now. Those fairymaids will grow tired of haunting me*, he thought, running the comb's teeth through his fingers

Beneath the clear blue waters of the Caribbean Sea, Mama D'Leau's anger was bubbling over like pepper pot stew. She could not understand how Pierre had resisted the fairymaid's dreams and now she was more furious than ever. "That foolish boy continues to use my magical golden comb. If he does not return it tonight, I will place a curse on the entire village!" she raged to her fairymaids.

That night, Pierre told his mother that he was going to the river, just as she'd advised him. "I'm going to return the golden comb of Mama D'Leau and ask the fairymaid to stop haunting me at night." His mother hugged him tightly, saying, "Thank you, my son. This is the right thing to do. We don't want any trouble to fall on our heads." She watched as he set off into the darkness of the night.

The moon was full, shining a sliver of light

through the trees. Pierre made his way through the mangroves, until he came to the part of the river where he had first found the golden comb. He stood at the edge of the water and called out, "Fairymaid, I've come to return Mama D'Leau's golden comb. Please release your hold on me."

In a short while, the fairymaid rose to the surface of the water. Her dark skin glistened in the moonlight as she swam over and sat on a nearby rock beside Pierre.

She stretched out her hand to Pierre. He walked up to her, but instead of handing her the comb, he took out his fishing net and threw it over the fairymaid, pulling it closed tightly. "Now I have caught you! You'll never haunt me again." She struggled and twisted in the net before shape-shifting into an angry black cat. Pierre jumped back in surprise and tried to hold on to the cat, who was hissing and clawing, but she shape-shifted into a small pool of water, trickling out of his hands and back into the river. At that moment, Pierre heard a loud cracking noise which sounded like a whip striking the water. He turned and saw a sea creature rising from the river. It was Mama D'Leau in all her fury. Her strands of hair were long venomous snakes, coiling around her face. She raised her serpent's tail and lashed it down on to the surface of the water, making the loud cracking sound that Pierre had heard. He stood frozen on the spot, too scared to run away. He held out the golden comb, which she snatched from his hands before speaking.

You dare to harm creatures that come from
the sea!
Now I will take you. Your life belongs to me.
You'll serve in my kingdom beneath the riverbed.
A mermaid you will be,
With a fish tail and a man's head.

Mama D'Leau snaked her giant tail around Pierre, squeezing his body tightly. He writhed and wriggled, trying desperately to get free, but it was no use. He was trapped by her power and strength. His limbs began to stiffen, his skin cracked and peeled, with scales forming on his legs. He soon realized that his body no longer belonged to him. Mama D'Leau cackled loudly with delight as she dragged him down deep into the river. Oh how he wished he hadn't tried to capture the fairy-maid. Further down they sank until they reached the bottom of the riverbed, where Mama D'Leau released her hold. Pierre was startled to see himself transform into a mermaid, with the upper body of a man and the tail of a mighty fish. He looked at his unusual body of glistening fins and scales, wondering what was to become of him now that he was a creature from the sea. He arched his back, letting his tail glide naturally through the water. Swishing gracefully in the water, swimming like a fish, he felt quite relieved, as if he was meant to be there. All of a sudden, the fairymaid appeared beside him. Her dark wavy hair flowed all around her and she smiled pleasantly.

"You belong with us now. Come with me," she said gently, and held his hand, leading him to their underwater kingdom filled with magical treasures. Pierre's eyes widened in surprise as more fairy-maids swarmed around to welcome him into their family of sea creatures.

"We are all fallen spirits who once crossed Mama D'Leau, but that is forgotten once you are here," announced one of the fairymaids. Her tail sparkled with all the colours of the sea, dazzling Pierre's eyes. He now understood that by helping to protect the rivers and the sea creatures, he would be forgiven for his past mistakes. In his new underwater home, he could live peacefully without the torment of his brothers from above the sea, under the rule of Mama D'Leau.

The Moongazer

Across the Caribbean countries, children are told about a giant ghostly figure that appears on the night of a full moon and scares everyone in the villages. In this version of the tale from Guyana, the Moongazer arrives and causes panic and destruction, until one brave girl saves the day.

Along the dark Essequibo River, there are hundreds of tiny islands, filled with coconut groves, waterfalls and rainforests crawling with wild animals. Slow-moving sloths, giant armadillos and white bearded capuchin monkeys play together in the forests.

On one of these small islands, a young girl named Cleo lived with her family in Parika village. She had walnut-coloured skin and wide eyes like an owl. Her five older brothers were stronger and taller than Cleo, but she was the most fearless. Whenever they explored in the forests and came across big cats prowling through the trees, Cleo was the one who would stand still whilst her brothers ran away. She held out her hands to the black-coated leopards and jaguars who came up to lick her palms. The animals never harmed or scared her.

Every day she and her friends went swimming in the rivers and creeks after school, to cool down from the sun's fierce heat. Sometimes they'd spot two large eyes floating in the water. "CROCODILE!" her friends would yell, swimming as fast as they could to the closest riverbank. But Cleo just giggled and splashed their long mouths. Then she'd sit on the crocodile's scaly back and ride the crocodile to shore.

Cleo wasn't only brave around wild animals. She had no fear of heights either. She'd climb up the tallest coconut tree and swing on their giant palms or jump from the highest waterfalls into fast-flowing rapids.

"Ayeeeeeeeeeee!" she'd scream out, diving all the way down with arms outstretched like a flying macaw.

One night, after a large supper of curry chicken and rice, Cleo and her family took their evening stroll. They'd often walk for miles alongside the Essequibo River. On this moonlit night, they passed the timber yard and the harbour, where ferry boats carried people between the islands. The bustling sounds from the market had died down as traders packed up their stalls. Cleo was strolling beside her mother, holding her hand, when they heard an ear-splitting scream and somebody shouting.

"RUN. EVERYBODY RUN!" People started scattering and bumping into each other, dropping their belongings. There was an unfamiliar sound of heavy stamping in the distance which shook the ground all around them. Cleo's family held on to each other, but no one knew which way to turn.

"What is happening?" Cleo asked her mother, but got no reply. She looked up and saw that fear had snatched her mother's voice, leaving her unable to speak. "We need to go home," she eventually managed to say, and tugged at Cleo's hand, forgetting how fearless her daughter always was. Cleo did not want to turn and run; she wanted to face whatever was there. As the rest of her family ran towards their home, she slipped away in the opposite direction and headed towards the sound of the stamping.

Further up ahead, stretched across the village rooftops, was the shadow of a tall, slim giant with dangling limbs. Lit up by the light of the moon, the shadow rippled along the buildings. Resting at the crossroads, the giant stood with hands on its hips. It gazed longingly up at the moon. Cleo turned the corner and first saw the giant's slender feet, which were the length of at least two boats. She looked up and stared at its legs, towering past the treetops. All around, buildings and homes had been flattened underneath the giant's feet. One man stopped to throw a chair at its legs; others threw rubbish and sticks, trying to injure it. But nothing worked. The giant just lifted its legs and stomped around angrily, trampling on bicycles and kicking over the clock tower.

"Child, you need to get away quickly. Don't stand there staring. If you walk between its legs, you'll get crushed." It was the voice of Mrs Daley, who ran the village bakery.

"What is it, Mrs Daley? What does it want?" Cleo asked, grabbing her by the hand. Mrs Daley wouldn't stop but managed to say, "It is a Moongazer, my child. Did your mother never tell you about them? Lost spirits making their way back to the moon." She hurried away, leaving Cleo thinking of the stories she'd been told. *I do remember Grandmother telling us about giants who are mesmerized by the moon, needing to reach out and touch it. She must have been speaking of the Moongazers!* Cleo's thoughts raced through her head excitedly. Rather than fear for her own safety, she was determined to help the giant reach the moon.

She watched as the Moongazer lifted up its long feet, leaving a white vapour rising up from the ground where it stood. It marched swiftly towards the river, crushing boats that were docked by the harbour. Cleo decided to act quickly. She ran as fast as she could to the tallest tree she could find.

Her nimble arms and legs moved swiftly up the trunk. She swung herself round as she'd seen the monkeys do, leaping from branch to branch until she reached the top. Her head poked out from the leaves, where she could see the path that the Moongazer had taken. Flattened homes, shops and trees snaked in a line like stepping stones throughout the village. Cleo could see that the giant was still not looking where it was going, only up at the moon. She put her fingers to her mouth and blew hard. A long high-pitched whistle came from her lips, catching the attention of the Moongazer. It looked down and straight at the tree where she was sitting. It began ripping up trees all around her, furiously hurling their trunks out of the way. Long, black tree roots dangled in the air, like giant, wriggly worms. She screamed out in terror thinking that her tree was going to be next. The Moongazer bent down and peered closely at Cleo. She could see the dark hollow shape of its eyes. There were tears streaming down its cheeks and misery was written all over its face. *This giant is sad and needs some help*, she thought. Then something utterly remarkable happened. The Moongazer, which had caused so much devastation, crushing and stomping everything in its path, uncaring how much damage it caused, reached out its long, narrow hand for Cleo to climb on to it. She jumped from the tree and into the Moongazer's palm, nestling down inside its shadowy hand. She thought back to the stories she'd heard from Grandmother and remembered one piece of advice: *Moongazers need to reach the highest ground and from there, they can gaze peacefully at the moon.* With this in her mind, Chloe tried to think of where the highest ground could be, and an idea slowly came to her of how she could help the giant.

"Follow my voice and I'll lead you to the moon," Cleo shouted as loud as she could into the Moongazer's ear. She guided it carefully, across the wide Essequibo River.

"Step over the islands," she said, hoping that no other villages or towns would be crushed. The Moongazer lifted its giant foot and stepped over Leguan Island, narrowly missing the schools, farms and animals. It placed its foot down into the water and then stepped over Wakenaam Island at the mouth of the river. People on the islands screamed out in terror as the Moongazer's jumbo feet hovered above, blocking out their sky. Everything on their islands was sent into complete darkness until the feet had passed over.

Cleo hung on to the edge of the Moongazer's fingers and led it along the rivers, to the highest peak on Cloud Mountain. White, fluffy clouds circled the tip of the mountain, with cool grey mist hovering all around. The Moongazer lowered Cleo safely on to the ground. It gave a wistful smile and then turned to face the moon. It stood gazing up into the sky longingly.

"You need to reach out to the moon!" cried Cleo, hoping that the Moongazer was powerful enough to get there. She watched as it leaped up high into the sky from the top of the mountains. Cleo saw the Moongazer's lithe body fly into the air, towards the moon. The silvery shadow disappeared into the night sky, where she hoped it found what it was looking for. Relieved that she had saved everyone from the Moongazer's heavy feet, she turned her thoughts towards heading home.

She was many miles away, and many large forests and islands now stood between her and her village, but she was not alone. Cleo turned to the birds who were soaring all around her. She grabbed hold of the feet of a yellow-beaked toucan, which carried her steadily down the mountain. Cleo glided through the air as if speeding down a wire and landed with a bump on the forest floor. There the red howler monkeys came to her aid, allowing her to grab hold of their tails and be swung from tree to tree. She raced through the forest, riding on the backs of leopards, and swam along the coast with dolphins and giant turtles. Before the end of the day, as the sun was disappearing behind the horizon, Cleo arrived back in Parika village.

"Where have you been?" screeched her mother when she saw Cleo strolling back into their home, tears rolling down her face. "We hoped the Moongazer had carried you away," laughed her brothers. Her family hugged and squeezed her tight, feeling such relief that she was back that they almost forgot to ask what had happened to the Moongazer. Once they had hugged her enough, they settled down to listen to her story. Her brothers teased her, not believing a word that she said. *Surely even she could not be that brave?* they all thought.

"Cleo, I don't know if your story is true. But I don't think it matters, do you? Whilst we were all running away, thinking of saving ourselves, you tried to find a solution," her mum said proudly, beaming at her fearless daughter. She didn't care whether Cleo had helped a giant. She was just happy to have her daughter safely back home with them all again.

Myths and Legends

The myths and legends from Africa are magical creation stories explaining how and why the world was shaped as it is. They are filled with powerful deities, formidable animals and the first people on our earth – heroes and heroines following their dreams and facing their nightmares. The landscapes are drawn from places that existed long ago or are still with us today. In these stories there is always a lesson to be learned.

How the World Was Created

(NIGERIA, TOGO & BENIN)

This creation myth is told among the Yoruba people from Nigeria, Togo and Benin in West Africa, where they tell stories of Orishas, deities who live in the sky. They are ruled by their creator, Olorun, who is known as their father, the sky god. This is the magical story of how "Obatala" created the earth, the first people and the first ancient city, Ife. Even though all of the Orishas have magical powers to create wonderful things, as you'll see in this story, their plans do not always work out as they expected.

Long, long ago, before the beginning of everything, there was only the sky up above and the water with wet marshlands down below. The vast blue sky was filled with a pantheon of *orishas* who were ruled by the father of the sky, a chief called Olorun. There were hundreds of these orishas living in the sky, each with their own strong personalities and powers. The sky was always full of arguments as the orishas fell out and clashed.

All the orishas had their own skills, and they lived peacefully together, dancing, singing, storytelling and feasting around a tall baobab tree. Obatala was the orisha of creativity and inner peace. He was a very deep thinker, always solving problems and coming up with ideas. One day, as he was sitting beside the tree, Olorun, father of the sky, noticed how quiet he was and tried to find out what was on his mind.

"Is anything troubling you, Obatala?" he asked. "You seem restless today."

Obatala sighed and stared up at the sky through the umbrella of branches stretched out above them. "I keep wondering if there is anything more that we orishas could do," he said.

"What do you mean? You have the entire sky to

explore, the universe at your powerful fingertips. Tell me, what more could you need?" Olorun prided himself on looking after all of his orisha children and wanted to help if he could.

Obatala assured him that he was very happy living in the sky, but he was curious about what else they could do with their powers. Olorun smiled knowingly. Obatala was always trying to improve himself. "You worry too much, Obatala. All is well," he said warmly. Feeling unsatisfied, and needing to think some more, Obatala took a stroll. He glided across the layer of powdery clouds, watching the sun streak pink colours across the sky. He stopped for a moment and peered down through the mist at the empty oceans below. *Surely we can make use of all that desolate space*, he thought to himself, and suddenly an idea came to him.

That evening over a delicious meal of *gbegiri* bean soup, Obatala shared his idea with Olorun. "Great father of the sky, I would like permission to journey beneath the clouds and visit the empty waters and wasteland below." His face glowed with excitement, matching the brightness of the sun.

"Whatever for? There is nothing there!" replied Olorun.

"Exactly!" said Obatala triumphantly. "I would like to use my powers to create dry land where all kinds of amazing creatures could grow and live. Then we could all put our powers to more use and help the creatures whenever they need it." His eyes sparkled like the stars at how clever his plan was. Olorun was very impressed, nodding his head enthusiastically.

"What a brilliant idea, Obatala. How noble of you to want to create and help others; of course you must do it," he said. Some of the other orishas felt inspired by his idea too. "You are so creative, Obatala. What a wonderful idea, I would love to assist you. I could spread love to those who desire it," said Oshun, who was responsible for love, fertility and abundance. "Be sure to ask for my help when you need to add a touch of beauty to your creations," she said pointedly. Oshun considered herself the most elegant of all the orishas and expected to be consulted on such matters.

"Of course," agreed Obatala. He knew better than to upset her. Although she was loving, she could be very spiteful if she felt insulted.

"Well, now that that is decided, you must first visit my eldest son, Orunmila, to find out what you will need for your mission," Olorun instructed, excited at the idea of a new world being made for the orishas to look after.

Orunmila was the orisha of wisdom and fate, a being cloaked in mystery and knowledge. He was able to tell the future of all who came to him. Obatala wandered around the universe searching for him and found him in the darkest corner of the sky, whispering with his close friend Eshu. Eshu was the mischievous messenger of the orishas, often playing sly tricks on everyone. He was so clever that he helped Orunmila work out how to translate all of his knowledge. Orunmila held so much wisdom and secrets about the universe in his mind but had no idea of what it all meant and how to share it in a helpful way. Once Eshu had befriended him, he helped him to interpret the meaning of all this knowledge and showed him a magical way of reading signs from trees and sand. Now Orunmila understood how to pass on wisdom to others if they asked.

"Good evening, Orunmila. I have come to ask for your help." Obatala bowed respectfully and then told of his plan to travel beneath the sky. "Please tell me what I will need for my journey," he said.

"Of course, Obatala. I will tell you what you need. First, I must look into the future for you." Orunmila prepared to read the divine signs and share his knowledge of what Obatala would need to do. He took out a long golden tray and sprinkled the powder of baobab roots on to it. The powder scattered across the tray in a flurry. Next he threw sixteen palm tree kernels on to the tray, which mingled with the powdered roots. With his dark brows furrowed, he looked carefully at where they landed and studied the patterns made in the powder. Obatala sat patiently whilst Orunmila did this eight times without saying a word. When he was finished, he looked up and said, "You will need a golden chain, long enough for you to climb down from the sky to the waters below. You must take a snail's shell filled with golden sand, a white hen, a black cat and a palm nut. All of these things will be useful for your mission."

Obatala looked confused. He had so many questions! "Why will I need all of those things? How will I take them with me? How will I stay above the water to create all living things?" he asked, slightly frustrated at Orunmila's cryptic message.

"Ask Ogun to build you a golden chain. Carry

the objects in a bag with you. The rest will become clear as you go." That was all Orunmila would tell him. "I am here for when you need help. That is all you need to know right now," he said, and sent him on his way.

So Obatala went to visit his son Ogun, the blacksmith who was very skilled at forging tools. Ogun was an enormous orisha with shoulders so broad he could block out the sun. His warrior legs were the size of giant tree trunks. The reason he was so muscled was because had to lift and bang heavy tools all day, making items that the orisha needed. He was probably strong enough to lift up a small planet. Most of his time was spent in a hot, dark workshop that always smelled of burning metal and gas. He never liked to be disturbed, especially if he was making something. And he was always making something. Obatala entered the workshop with trepidation, not wanting to disturb his son. He felt his nostrils burning from the smell of hot metal. He came face to face with a huge blast of heat from a firepit. Ogun was banging a piece of hot iron with a heavy hammer.

CLANG CLANG CLANG SCREEEEEECH. The

hammer made a terrific noise as it hit the iron. Orange sparks flew out and scattered around the room.

"SORRY," shouted Obatala.

CLANG

"TO—"

CLANG CLANG

"INTERRUPT YOU," he yelled above the sound of tools being struck.

Ogun remained hunched over his iron anvil, crafting a long machete.

"I NEED YOU—"

BANG BANG TIIIING

"TO MAKE ME—"

SCREEEEEEEEECH

"A LONG—"

TICK TICK SCRAAAATCH

"GOLDEN CHAIN," pleaded Obatala, totally exasperated.

"CAN YOU HEAR ME?"

CLINK CLINK CLANG CLANG. Ogun continued to strike the hot metal with his hammer.

"IT NEEDS TO BE LONG ENOUGH—"

RATTLE CLATTER CLATTER.

Obatala felt all his nerves twitching from the sounds. He continued.

"TO REACH FROM THE SKY TO THE WATERS BELOW," he shouted as quickly as he could.

"Bring me the gold and I'll make it for you," replied Ogun gruffly without looking up or stopping his banging.

"HOW MUCH GOLD SHALL I BRING?" asked Obatala.

"Enough to fill that," Ogun said, and pointed in the corner to a ginormous three-legged cauldron. Obatala was speechless. The cauldron was huge. *Yes, I am clever, and yes, I am powerful*, he thought, *but where will I find enough gold to fill that massive pot?* He didn't have any to hand and it wasn't like there were great big piles of gold just sitting around in the sky.

Obatala muttered his thanks and left the workshop. He made his way back to the great baobab tree, where Shango was drumming a fast rhythm on his batá, a double-headed drum. Oya, his wife, was spinning around, dancing wildly. Her orange-flamed dress floated behind her as she held on to its sides. Many of the orishas joined in, singing and dancing to the beat of the drum.

Gbe ẹsẹ rẹ jo, jo!
Move your feet and dance, dance!

They threw their arms in the air and bent their knees, jumping from side to side. Obatala relaxed at the root of the tree, watching them. He loved it when everyone danced. Their bright robes were magnificent shades of red, blue, orange and green. They flew through the sky as they danced, like a flock of tropical birds. Suddenly Obatala noticed their heavy golden jewellery shimmering against their dark skin. Rows of golden necklaces, headbands, bracelets and armbands were clasped around their bodies. *All of us orishas are covered in gold. I can put them all together!* he thought, and realized where he could get enough gold to make his chain ladder.

Obatala went rushing to Ogun's workshop the next morning, laden with piles of gold. He'd begged the orishas to give him their jewellery and they were happy to help.

"Here you are!" he announced proudly, and dropped all of the gold at his son's feet. Ogun was hanging new weapons he had made on his walls. He turned around and looked down at all the gold

"Thank you, Father. This will be enough. Your chain will be ready tomorrow at sunrise." He scooped up the glittering pile of metal and placed it in the giant cauldron, ready to melt into liquid gold.

The next morning, Obatala prepared to set off below the sky, armed with his enormous golden chain, a snail shell filled with sand, a white hen, a black cat and a palm nut in his canvas bag. A few of the orishas turned up to see him leave. Some of them, like Orunmila, wanted to be around in case he needed any help. Others, like Eshu, turned up out of curiosity, expecting something to go drastically wrong. Obatala hung the end of the chain on to the corner of the sky and started to climb down. The air was cool and still, floating silently around him. He climbed through galaxies of stars and purple dust clouds. He moved past planets circling the sun. He climbed for seven days and seven nights until he reached the last step on the chain. He looked down and saw that the swirling blue water was still very far away. The golden chain was not long enough for him to reach it. He clung on to the chain, balancing between the sky and the water.

He called out to Orunmila, "The chain is not long enough. What shall I do?" Orunmila was waiting up above and heard his voice loud and clear.

"Obatala!" cried out Orunmila. "Pour out the sand from the snail's shell and release the white hen."

Obatala did as he was instructed. He tipped the golden sand out from the shell. As soon as it touched the water, it spread and formed dry land. He released the white hen, who flapped its wings and landed softly on the dry land. She pecked around on the ground, scattering the sand. It blew and grew into piles of sand which magically formed sloping mountains, hills and valleys. Obatala looked down below and saw that he was near the land. He jumped from the end of the chain and landed on the newly formed earth.

"This place where I have landed shall be called *Ife. The place that divides waters*," he decided. The dry land stretched out as far and wide as he could see. Obatala walked around, exploring the dry land.

Now it is time to create and turn the land green with living things, he thought. He reached into his bag and pulled out the brown palm nut and planted it in the ground. The nut sprouted roots which took hold in the earth. Soon a green bud popped out and grew instantly into a magnificent flowering palm tree. Its dark green leaves fanned out like feathers around the clumps of hanging nuts. Obatala's eyes opened wide with wonder as he watched the tree drop more palm nuts on to the ground. These nuts scattered and grew into palm trees, which dropped more seeds that grew into new trees. The process kept repeating until a large area of land was covered with long, slender tree trunks, all crisscrossed and knobbly, towering into the sky, casting shade in all directions. The black cat purred and brushed against Obatala's legs whilst they strolled across the land together. They kept each other company over the next few months, whilst he was magically creating.

As the sun warmed the earth each day, nature sprang to life and more beautiful wildlife appeared. Golden-winged dragonflies hovered in the air. Giant forest geckos slept in the shade. Carpets of white lily flowers blossomed on the hills. Everywhere was full of colour and life.

But one morning, Obatala looked around and felt that something was still missing from his creation. After walking through the hot day, he sat by a stream and leaned over to drink some of the water. His reflection stared back at him. His dark brown eyes blinked when he blinked. His white teeth glistened when he smiled. His white robes moved when he moved. *That's what's missing*, he thought to himself. *Someone who looks like me. Someone who can keep me company.* Without thinking, Obatala began to play with the clay at the edge of the stream. He started moulding and shaping it with the water. His hands moved quickly and very soon he created a figure that looked just like he did. He carried on moulding the clay figures, in all shapes and sizes. There were tall people, short people, men, women, babies, and children. After a while he grew tired and stopped for a break. He squeezed some sap from a palm tree flower to quench his thirst. It was so delicious and sweet that he couldn't stop drinking it. The flavour was new to him and he did not realize that the juice was fermented and turning to alcohol. Obatala was drinking palm wine, which made him dizzy and drunk. "Time to make more clay people," he sang out loud, and stumbled back to the clay. He carried on moulding new people but because he had drunk so much wine, he could not control his fingers very well and he found it hard to concentrate on his task. Some of the clay figures had missing eyes and limbs or misshapen bodies. When the effects of the palm wine wore off, Obatala looked over his work. He saw that the new clay figures had come out differently, but he loved that they were more interesting and unique than the others. He admired his own handiwork but decided he would not drink any more palm wine so that he could stay focused on his tasks.

Later that evening, Obatala noticed a brown chameleon with bulging eyes, hanging upside down on the branch of a tree. He did not remember creating one and asked where he came from. He crawled down from the tree and sat near Obatala.

"Olorun sent me to check on your progress," replied the lizard, changing from brown to green, matching the grass. "Show me what you have created," he said. So Obatala pointed out the land and all of the wildlife. He showed him the trees and plants, the hills and valleys. He showed him all of the people he had moulded and shaped in his own image.

"You have done well, Obatala. Why do you look so disappointed? It seems you are not quite happy," said the chameleon.

Obatala sighed and explained how sad he was that the figures he created looked like him but had no life. "They are not living and breathing beings like me."

The chameleon went back to Olorun in the sky and told of Obatala's creations and how, despite all he had done, he was disappointed. Olorun was impressed with what Obatala had achieved and knew exactly how he could help. He gathered lots of gasses from around the sky and sparked them into a huge fireball. He tossed the exploding fire down to earth and blew his mighty breath on to it. The fireball spread across the land, heating up the ground and turning it into solid earth. The red-hot flames baked the clay figures, breathing life into the moulded shapes. They became living and breathing people, just like Obatala. But that's not all the fireball changed. It landed on the earth with such a powerful force, that it sent Obatala's new land spinning into the sky, and there the earth still spins today, moving around the sun.

The people Obatala had created came together to form the first city on earth. The ancient city of Ife, which prospers and flourishes in Nigeria today.

How Death Came to the World

(UGANDA)

This myth is a creation story about the Buganda people of Uganda in East Africa. In this version, Kintu is the first man to be created on earth. When he meets and falls in love with Nambi, the sky god's daughter, he is set several impossible challenges to prove if he is worthy to marry her.

A long, long time ago, before the beginning of time, the god Gulu, creator of all things, ruled in the sky. His children spent their days racing around the universe, leaping across stars and dancing through galaxies. They made up magical games and sometimes raced each other across the sky, moving at the speed of light. Their dark bodies glistened with a bright glow all around them and their strong arms could stretch over trees or carry the weight of a mountain. Their father's golden palace of many rooms, stretched right across the sky. Surrounded by lakes of many colours and enormous plants bursting with fragrance, it was a delightful place to be.

One day, Gulu's only daughter, Nambi, a fiery, fearless goddess, went to play hide-and-seek on earth with two of her brothers, Kiwanuka and Kayiikuuzi. They slid down a giant rainbow which stretched across the sky right down to earth. They glided along its bright colours and landed in the country of Uganda. They were surrounded by green valleys and lakes with clear waters which looked almost as beautiful as their home in the sky. Here on earth there was vast open space which they did not have to share with the other gods in the sky. It was their giant playground which they loved having all to themselves. Nambi and her brothers spent the day darting through forests and swimming in the lakes, until the sun slowly disappeared behind the hills.

"Catch this moonbeam," Nambi yelled to her brother, and threw him a ray of light from the moon to brighten up their way. He caught it swiftly and held it up high, showering light across the low valley of hills. It was night-time on earth and the darkness made their game of hide-and-seek even more fun. Nambi ran into a forest of trees and found a cave to hide in. It was so dark and cosy inside that she soon fell asleep. Her brothers grew so bored of searching for their sister that they returned to their home in the sky. They knew that she would come home when she was ready.

When Nambi woke up, she stood up and immediately bumped into something large and soft. She ran her fingers across the surface where it felt furry and warm to the touch. She did not recognize it and was curious to find out what this could be. It was not until she heard it cry out "MOOOOOOO" that she realized it was a cow. At this time, the earth was only filled with shrubs and trees. There were no animals as far as Nambi knew.

What is a cow doing on earth? she wondered, and started to look around for more signs of life. After walking out of the cave, she heard a loud snore coming from a tree just ahead. Fearless as always, Nambi tiptoed up to the tree, not wanting to stir whatever was sleeping beside it. On a bed of entwined leaves, nestled beneath the tree's branches, a man was sleeping peacefully. Nambi stopped abruptly, standing as still as she could, and stared. She had never seen a human before. His skin was as dark as midnight and his hair twisted and curled into tight knots around his head.

Hearing someone moving near him, the man woke up and stared in amazement at Nambi. He knew instantly that she was immortal. She was draped in stiff cloth woven from the bark of the mutuba tree and wore golden sandals on her feet. Her bronzed skin glistened in the darkness and her black eyes flashed with flecks of amber, as if she could set fire to him with just one nod of her head. He was a little bit terrified, not knowing what to do, so he bowed his head and greeted her respectfully.

"Hello, divine child of Gulu. My name is Kintu."

Nambi was impressed with his manners. He was

far more polite than her unruly brothers, who teased her every day.

"What are you doing here on this earth?" she asked. Her voice echoed with power, encouraging Kintu to speak more.

He stood up proudly and replied, "I am the first man who was created, living here on earth with my cow." She smiled warmly and he couldn't wait to tell Nambi all about himself. Night drifted slowly into day whilst they carried on getting to know each other.

"You live here all alone with just a cow for company?" Nambi found this hilarious. "What do you talk about?" She could barely stop laughing at her own question. Kintu laughed too and tried to think of what he said to his cow most days.

"I say, good morning, my dear cow. How are you today?" He stepped forward and bowed, showing how he greeted his cow. She giggled uncontrollably, imitating his greeting. She was having so much fun that she soon forgot that she was meant to return to her home in the sky. Kintu was attentive, listening to all that she had to say, unlike her unruly brothers. He found her to be bright and engaging with lots of stories to share. He loved to hear her laugh;

it was so infectious. Their smiles reached their eyes and they found themselves giggling at each other. Then his smile disappeared and his eyes fell to the ground.

"I did not realize how lonely I was until I met you, Nambi." They both stopped laughing and sat in silence. Nambi felt very sorry for Kintu, living all alone on earth. He confessed that he longed for someone to keep him company. She wished she could stay longer but she knew her family would be anxious. Later that day she turned to him and said, "I must return to my family in the sky. I have stayed far too long. My father, Gulu, will be worried."

Kintu was greatly saddened by this news. He had fallen in love with Nambi and did not want her to go.

"Please stay here and marry me," he begged, holding her hand to his heart. She beamed with delight, flooded with joy at his proposal. But suddenly, her face clouded over as she thought about what her father would say.

"I would love to stay here with you, Kintu, but first I must speak with my father and ask for his blessing to marry you." She hugged him tightly and said goodbye.

"I promise to return soon," she sang, flying swiftly into the sky like a golden eagle.

"I promise to wait right here," he called back, with hope rising in his voice. He watched sorrowfully as Nambi disappeared, leaving a trail of golden stardust behind her.

When she arrived back home, Gulu was seated on his throne in the clouds, waiting to hear why Nambi had remained on earth overnight. He was cross that her brothers had left his daughter alone.

"Nambi, my golden child, what have you been doing all alone on earth?"

"Father, I have so much to tell you. I met the only man on earth and we talked all day and all night." Her words tumbled together and her face shone with love and excitement. Gulu's brow deepened when she continued to tell him of her love for Kintu and their plans to marry and live together in Uganda. Her father was not pleased at all.

"We do not know this Kintu. He is not a god like you! He has nothing but a cow to his name! How can he be worthy of my daughter?" Gulu's dark eyes burned with fury. His son Walambe, who was always miserable and gloomy, joined in the conversation, siding with their father.

"You could never be happy with a man and his cow," he sneered.

Each of the brothers saw this as a chance to throw their questions and comments from all directions.

"He is not like us."

"What will you do on earth?"

"How will you live?"

"Does he only have one cow?"

"Why do you want to leave us?"

"You will miss us."

"Can he wrestle?"

"Can he fly?"

The questions came tumbling out of their mouths like running water. Nambi did not have a moment to answer. While his sons were talking, Gulu sat thinking. How could he make sure his beautiful daughter didn't marry someone he hadn't chosen?

After a few moments, Gulu ordered everyone to be quiet. He had come to a decision.

"I will give you my blessing to marry this Kintu person, if he can pass my test." Gulu smiled broadly, believing that no human could ever pass one of his divine tests. Nambi's brothers all cheered, agreeing this was the best way to see if Kintu was worthy to be her husband. Nambi was furious and tried to argue with her father. She thought the idea was unfair. *How could Kintu pass a test set by Gulu, the creator?* She stormed off, stamping across the sky, darkening the clouds as she went. Despite all of her raging and reasoning, Nambi had no choice but to accept her father's decision. Kintu was going to be tested, and if he truly wanted to marry her, he would have to surpass her father's expectations.

One of her brothers was sent to fetch Kintu and his cow from earth. When he arrived in their kingdom in the sky, his eyes widened at all the beauty and opulence which surrounded him. Animals of all shapes and sizes roamed freely on the sloping hills. Tall trees hung down low. Their branches almost touched the ground from the weight of their giant fruits. Cascading waterfalls changed colours, right before his eyes. Purple, turquoise and yellow water poured down into glittering lakes. As he entered their palace, Kintu saw walls covered with precious stones, shining brightly in every room. Kintu lived a humble life on earth with his cow and had never seen such wealth and abundance before. Awed and amazed, he was brought before Gulu and knelt at the creator's feet, where he sat on his throne the colour of sunset gold.

"Welcome, Kintu, first man on earth," Gulu's voice boomed loudly around the room. He towered above Kintu, wearing a long white kanzu robe.

"Before you can marry my daughter, you must first pass a test to prove your worth. You will be invited to eat a royal banquet. Every morsel of food must be eaten, to prove you are Nambi's equal." Kintu nodded and sighed in relief. This sounded like a simple task which he could pass easily. *What was Nambi so worried about?* he thought to himself.

The brothers stood around their father, smirking and elbowing each other, trying to smother their laughter. Nambi ignored them but felt suspicious. She did not trust her brothers or her father and wondered what tricks they were up to. She watched worriedly as Kintu was led into one of the dining rooms in their palace in the clouds. He was seated in the middle of a long table, shimmering with moon dust and starlight. The table was so huge that Kintu could not see where it began or ended. Someone entered the room carrying a platter of fresh fruits. Giant chunks of juicy pineapple, slices of sweet mango, bananas, passion fruit and jackfruit were piled up high in front of him. Kintu had never seen such a variety of fruits.

On earth he only had cow's milk to drink! He rubbed his hands in delight.

This challenge is going to be easy. I will enjoy eating all of this wonderful food, Kintu thought and was just about to dive into the food when the door opened again and someone else entered the room. They were carrying a platter of vegetables, which they placed in front of him. Steaming-hot sweet potatoes, yams, cassava, pumpkin and beans sat waiting to be eaten. Before Kintu could ask any questions, the door opened again and another platter was brought in, then another and another and another until there were over a hundred platters of food covering the table. This was Kintu's test. He was expected to eat all the food that had been given to him. *What am I going to do? It is impossible for me to eat all of this food by myself*, Kintu thought, horrified. He sat there alone, with his head in his hands, trying to come up with an idea for how to manage all the food.

When Nambi saw all of the food being carried to Kintu, she knew that her father and brothers had set him up to fail. *I must help him!* she thought, and quickly came up with a plan. Without anyone seeing, Nambi called out to the ants in their kingdom, who came to her immediately. A long line of fiery red ants stamped their feet towards her. They gathered eagerly around her golden sandals.

"How can we serve you? Tell us what you need," squeaked the ants. She bent down and whispered what she wanted them to do. They instantly formed a single line and marched off at top speed. The ants crawled into the room where Kintu was eating. They climbed up the legs of the giant table and spread themselves all over the food. Kintu watched in amazement as the ants collected every morsel of food, placed it on their backs and ran away back down their hole. When Gulu entered the room to see how Kintu was getting on, he saw that all of the food platters were empty. He was very shocked and almost lost for words.

"My my, what a mighty man you are. You have passed my test and eaten all of my enormous feast." He praised Kintu loudly, whilst Nambi's brothers stood in silence, their mouths open wide in disbelief. Nambi's face glowed with pride. No one suspected that she had helped Kintu. Now she hoped they could go and live on earth together.

"Seeing as you have passed this test so easily, I would like you to take another test," said Gulu, to

Kintu's dismay. But Gulu was the creator, after all. He could change the rules whenever he wanted. The brothers chuckled and tried to hide their smiles. This time, they thought Kintu was sure to fail. Nambi folded her arms and glared at her father. She was afraid of the next impossible challenge he was going to set for Kintu.

"Here is my bronze axe. I would like you to make firewood from rocks. That is what I need for my fire."

Kintu took the axe from Gulu and wondered how he could cut rocks with it. *The rocks will surely chip the metal blade.* He was told to return to the palace with a basketful of finely sliced rocks. Kintu stood at the foot of a steep mountain and raised his bronze axe, preparing to hit the solid rock. He closed his eyes, certain that the blade would split in two. Nambi watched from a distance and raised her hands to her lips. She blew a kiss filled with powerful magic which landed on the bronze tip of the axe. As Kintu swung his arms down low with all his strength, the tip of the axe sliced through the rock, making it break away smoothly.

"What is happening?" cried Kintu. He could not believe his eyes as the axe cut the rock into small logs of stone. Delighted, he filled his basket with the freshly cut stones and returned to Gulu, where he was waiting with all of his sons. Again, they were surprised that Kintu had passed the second test. Each brother began to wonder if Kintu perhaps was a mighty man after all.

"Now surely you have tested Kintu enough?" Nambi stood with her hands on her hips, questioning her father. But Gulu was still not quite convinced that Kintu deserved to marry his daughter.

"I have one last test for Kintu. I want him to fill this bucket with water." He smiled warmly and handed Kintu a golden bucket. Finally, this seemed like a simple task, thought Kintu with relief. But Gulu carried on speaking.

"I do not drink water from the well. I only drink fresh morning dew. That is what you must fill the bucket with," he instructed Kintu, and sent him on his way. Kintu walked towards a purple lake floating in the sky. He sat beneath a tree and closed his eyes, trying to think of how he could pass this test. If only he could just fill his bucket with water from the lake. He was deep in thought when suddenly he heard a dripping noise beside him.

Drip, drip, drop, drop. It was very slow at first and

then gradually picked up speed. *Drip drip drip drip, drop drip drop drip.* Kintu opened his eyes and saw that he was surrounded by colourful butterflies. Their bright, velvety wings fluttered all around him. Nambi, looking on from afar, had sent them to help with this last task. The butterflies gathered together, hovering over the blades of grass and long leaves. They used their delicate arms to collect large droplets of dew and brought them to the bucket. Soon the bucket was filled to the top with fresh morning dew. Kintu was overjoyed. He sprang up from the ground and dashed back to Gulu, who thought that Kintu had given up by now.

"Here is your bucket of fresh morning dew," said Kintu proudly, handing him the bucket. Gulu was finally impressed. He had no idea how Kintu had overcome all of these challenges, but he did not care. He was happy.

"You have surprised me, Kintu, and shown that you are indeed worthy to walk among us. You and Nambi shall both have my blessing to marry and live on earth." Nambi sighed in relief and hugged her father.

Gulu knew that earth was mostly wilderness with only a few trees, valleys and lakes. He did not want Nambi to be lonely or have hardship. He wanted them to create more life so that people and animals could grow and flourish.

"Take these things with you. They will help you start a new life." Gulu handed them bananas, potatoes, beans, millet, groundnuts, and a hen.

"Thank you, Father. I will pack my belongings and then say goodbye to my brothers," Nambi said. Gulu shook his head and suddenly looked horrified.

"When you leave, you must not let your brother Walambe see you. You know how he loves to follow you everywhere. He will want to go with you." Nambi looked sad, but she knew that this was good advice. Kintu was confused; he did not understand Gulu's words.

"Why does it matter if Walambe follows us?" he asked Nambi.

"My brother's name means *death*. He cannot help it, but he often causes misery and disease wherever he goes. Sometimes he gets left out of our adventures because things may die if he is there. He will not be happy about me leaving him behind." Nambi prepared to leave, but Gulu had one last piece of advice to offer his daughter. "When you leave, do not come back. Even if you forget something, do not return for it. You must make sure Walambe does not see you." Nambi nodded happily and then hurried away to pack her belongings.

The clouds hung heavy with a shower of rain, ready to pour down and water the earth. Kintu and Nambi reached the edge of the sky and were about to slide down a long rainbow when she remembered something.

"I forgot to bring the millet for the hen!" she shrieked. "I must go and get it. There will be nothing on earth for the hen to eat." Kintu held her hands and begged her to leave it behind. "Remember what your father said. Do not go back for anything."

Nambi was not worried and felt sure that she could slip away unseen. "I will go swiftly; Walambe will not see me." She tried to reassure Kintu. She dashed back to her home and grabbed the millet. Just as she was leaving, she heard a familiar voice.

"Where are you going, Nambi?" It was Walambe, and he sounded very unhappy. He stood with his arms hanging loosely at his sides. His head hung down low with great sadness.

"I'm going to earth, Walambe. I am going with Kintu."

"Let me come too," he pleaded, and inched his feet towards her.

"No, Walambe. Do not ask me." She turned to leave but Walambe followed. He shuffled slowly behind her. She stopped and turned around. He stopped and stood still. Nambi carried on walking and Walambe continued to follow. His long feet dragged noisily on the ground. She stopped and turned around. He stopped and stood still.

"Walambe! Stop following me." She started to run and so did he. Kintu saw her coming with Walambe closely behind her.

"Why have you brought your brother?" Kintu moaned. Nambi said she was sorry but there was nothing she could do.

"No one ever wants me around," wailed Walambe, glaring at them both.

"OK, Walambe, you can come with us to earth, but only for a little while, and then you must return to Gulu, here in the sky." Nambi hoped this would make him feel better.

Together, they all fell to earth to create their new homes. Nambi asked Walambe to live on a mountainside where he would not cause too much trouble. She showed Kintu how to plant mutuba trees so that they could make bark cloth. They planted plantain trees and all of the seeds and vegetables Gulu had given them. After a while the land blossomed with plantain, lemon, mango and papaya trees. Everywhere was green and full of life. Kintu and Nambi lived happily and soon had their own children.

Walambe mostly stayed away on the mountainside. Whenever he visited during the dry season, the plants would wither and die and the animals would become sick. Poor Nambi and Kintu had to begin their planting all over again. After this happened a few times, Nambi told Walambe that it was time for him to return to the sky.

"No. Why should I go back?" Walambe refused. He was happy on earth, where no one bothered him, and did not want to leave. Nambi tried to explain that he was ruining the earth, but that made him more angry.

"Seeing as you don't want me here, I will stay for ever!" He stamped his foot and caused the earth to crack and shake with his rage. With that, Walambe vanished from their home and hid in the centre of the earth, refusing to go back to his father's kingdom in the sky.

Gulu learned of Walambe's behaviour and sent Nambi's other brother Kayiikuuzi to capture him. Kayiikuuzi's name meant *digger* and so he was able to dig deep very fast, right down into the centre of the earth to search for Walambe. Kayiikuuzi tried very hard, but every time he got close to Walambe, he disappeared, leaving only signs of sickness and disease. The chase went on for years. By now, many people were living in Uganda and they all saw signs of the quarrelling brothers. Walambe would appear and something or someone would die. Kayiikuuzi would appear and almost catch him, leaving huge holes in the ground from all of his digging.

Finally, one morning, Nambi had had enough. She stood in front of their home and called out, loud and clear to summon both of her brothers.

"WALAMBE! KAYIIKUUZI!" Her voice was filled with the strength of the sky and everyone, everywhere heard it. Both of her brothers came and stood sulkily before her.

"There is to be no more destruction to the earth. Stop running and chasing each other. Go back to the sky or stay here in peace." She stared angrily at them both and waited for a reply.

"I am sorry, Nambi. Gulu asked me to fetch

Walambe but I will go back and tell him I tried my best." Kayiikuuzi twisted and turned with the speed of a hurricane, flying up high into the sky. Walambe stared at the ground, ashamed to meet his sister's eyes.

"I'm sorry too, Nambi. I don't want to leave. I want to stay with you here on earth," he said, hoping that she would not banish him.

Her face softened a little and she thought of a compromise that might work for them both.

"I will let you stay on earth, but you are to remain hidden from all humans and only visit once every full moon. This will give us time to recover from your visit," she said.

"Thank you, my sister," said Walambe, delighted with this plan as it meant he could still see his sister. He shuffled away and vanished into the forest.

The people and wildlife of Uganda continued to live happily and grow, learning how their ancestors first came to their world. Every so often when someone would become sick or die, they knew that Walambe, *death*, had visited them.

Why the Sun is Brighter than the Moon

(CAMEROON)

In this beautiful creation story from the Wuté people of Cameroon, the sun and the moon were friends who once shone with equal brightness in the sky until the Sun tricked the Moon and the two parted ways.

Before the beginning of time, the Sun and the Moon shone as brightly as each other in the vast sky. They were the best of friends, always marvelling at each other's brilliance. Sun was radiant and created a wonderful warmth, which spread throughout the land. She shone brightly with her children who were small sunrays of light, flickering around her. All the animals and people on earth were warmed by Sun's gaze and felt joy and happiness when she was around. Rainforest trees grew thick and tall, eagerly stretching towards her light.

In contrast, Moon was graceful with a silvery shimmer which reflected upon anyone in her presence. Big cats loved how their fur glistened from the light of the moon. Rivers and seas showed off their silver waves when Moon was near. Bats swooped low, watching their wings form shadows in Moon's light. Moon had children just like Sun. They were formed in her image and sprinkled across the sky, glittering all around her.

Sun was quite a playful girl, dancing around the earth during the day. She'd glide gracefully across the sky and tease her friends to come out and play.

"Come on, Wind, come on, Rain! Let's create a storm and streak the sky with colourful rainbows," she'd say, giving an extra big smile to grey Fog, who always looked a bit sulky. Wind would huff and puff, asking the clouds to release the rain. Lightning would crack her thunderbolts, sending bright flashes of light into the sky. But Moon would sit quietly in a corner, rarely joining in. She preferred to watch their games from her side of the sky. She was always friendly but a little bit cool with everyone, keeping a polite distance. Sun found this extremely irritating. She was used to everyone enjoying her company, revelling in her warmth. Sometimes it angered her that she had to share the sky with Moon at all.

"If you don't want to play, go and sit somewhere else so I can shine brightly all by myself," she'd say, blazing her rays in Moon's direction. They had equal space in the sky, but Sun was fed up of sharing and wanted the space all to herself. Early one morning, she decided to do something about it. Just as the earth was waking up, Sun called out across the sky to Moon.

"Let's go and relax in the Benue River. We can gently lower ourselves into the water and cool off for a while," she said, dazzling Moon with one of her best smiles.

"That's a great idea," said Moon. She thought it would be nice for them to spend time together, and the river was wide enough for them to bathe in. Sun wanted to dip into the river first.

"Once you see the water getting hot from my warm sunrays, it means I am ready for you to join me in the water," said Sun. But Sun had more than a pleasant swim on her mind. She was planning to trick Moon.

Slowly, she dipped her rays beneath the clouds, lowering herself past the lush green mountains until she came to the canopy of trees. When Moon's eyes were looking elsewhere, Sun signalled to her children and whispered instructions to them.

"Come quickly. Use your sunbeams to set fire to those branches and throw the hot twigs into the river!"

She then drifted out of sight and hid near a bend in the river. Sun's children lightly touched the edges of a tree, setting fire to the branches with their heat. As soon as their orange flames danced along the twigs, the children grabbed them and tossed them into the river, just as their mother had told them to. The river water began to bubble and boil from the hot twigs, warming up the water.

"Ah, I can see the steam rising up from the river. Sun must have dipped into it," said Moon, starting to glide down and enter the water too. As soon as she was comfortably nestled beneath the surface of the water, Moon's silver glow began to fade. She suddenly grew dull and pale as the hot water drained her shine. Sun hovered from her hiding place and smiled smugly at her deception.

"Oh no, what is happening?" cried out Moon, watching her shimmer melt into the water. She saw Sun's smile and realized immediately what had happened.

"Sun, I thought you were in the water too! How could you trick me in this cruel way? Now my silver glow has disappeared. I will never shine again."

"You will still shine, just not as brightly as me," Sun snapped back, barely able to hide her pleasure.

Moon gathered herself and rose back into the clear blue sky, feeling sad and humiliated. Now, whenever she sat alongside the Sun during the day, she could hardly be seen. She had faded away to a faint, silvery outline. Ashamed that she had now lost her bright glow, she only crawled out at night-time when Sun was asleep. Now no one could match Sun's radiance and power during the day.

She alone could make the flowers bloom, the trees rise up and the people come out of their homes with smiles.

But Sun's constant warmth made the earth too hot and fires broke out around the world, wiping out many forests. People on the earth cut down the trees, but that made the earth even hotter. Sun watched in despair as humans forgot how to look after their earth, creating toxic pollution which rose up into the sky.

Sun gathered all of her friends to help slow down the destruction that was taking place down below.

"Come out, Wind, Rain, Thunder and Lightning! We need to join forces and play more together. The earth needs our help to survive." But Wind did not like all the smelly fumes rising into the air from the earth, so she would not come out and play. And Rain did not like being bossed around by Sun so he would not pour water on fires that erupted from the earth.

"Leave us alone, Sun. We don't want to play all the time," grumbled Wind, storming off in a huff.

"You wanted to shine by yourself so now is your chance," said Rain, haughtily. And they drifted away, leaving Sun to burn hotter and hotter on to the earth. Moon watched quietly from her corner of the sky as people around the world began to suffer and die. She saw famines break out across lands where it was too hot for food to grow. She heard animals in the north and south pole shrieking in horror as their icy mountains began to melt. *Sun's heat was reaching all the cold areas of the world!* she thought sadly. Moon covered her eyes when forest fires broke out and spread furiously across the lands, burning down homes and forests.

The world is in chaos and it is partly Sun's fault. She's so selfish and greedy, thought Moon. She seethed with anger, remembering how Sun had tricked her in the river, and came up with an idea of how to get revenge.

One night, just before Sun dipped down below the earth, Moon turned to her and said, "Our children of moonbeams and sunrays are suffering from all of this pollution rising high into the sky. Their lights are fading and they are choking from all the toxic fumes."

"You are right, Moon. I hate seeing our children suffer in this way. Soon they will disappear from all of the earth's pollution. But there is nothing we can do," Sun said with tears in her eyes.

"I have an idea, but you might not like it," said Moon, pretending to look concerned. She hoped that Sun would not suspect her trickery.

"What is it? I am willing to try anything," Sun asked eagerly.

"We should end the lives of our children so that they are spared from any more pain." Her eyes filled with tears as she spoke. Sun was shocked at first and would not agree.

"No no no no no. We cannot do that," cried Sun, turning away. But as the years drifted by with more famines and fires, Sun started to warm to Moon's idea. She was heartbroken at the thought but knew she could no longer bear to see her children of glistening sunbeams shrivel away slowly. *It would be better for me to put out their light than have them suffer like this*, she thought sorrowfully, and turned to Moon, saying, "I have changed my mind after seeing more devastation on the earth and in the sky. Let us stop our children's suffering and put out their light, but you must do it first."

Moon smiled slyly, feeling pleased that her trick was starting to work. She agreed to gather her children first and place them in the river to end their glowing light. She told Sun that when she saw the river flow silver with her children's light, that meant her children were gone and it was Sun's turn.

The following morning, before Sun had risen to take her place in the sky, Moon travelled across the earth and shone her light on the steepest mountain-side. Her shimmer melted the rocks, transforming them into clay which slithered into the river. The clay mixed with the water, changing its colour from grey to silver. When Sun woke up and saw the river glowing pearly white, she assumed it was the light from Moon's children. With a heavy heart, she gathered her own children around her and blew out their light. With one stroke, they were all gone. Only Sun's light shone in the sky. When it was time for Sun to set, Darkness crept out sleepily, ready for night-time to begin. Sun was about to close her eyes when she saw Moon's children scattered across the sky. They were still there, shining brightly all around their mother.

"How are your children still here?" Sun screamed at Moon when she realized that her children were still alive. "I saw the river flowing pearly white! I thought you had dimmed their light. How could you trick me in this cruel way?" Sun was devastated and blistered with rage, burning and howling into the night sky. She howled all night, until finally Darkness tiptoed away, ready for Sun to take over.

Sun had spent the night, pondering about her own behaviour and why Moon tricked her. Grumpily she looked over at Moon, who was resting in her corner.

"I'm sorry for tricking you into dimming your light in the river, Moon. It was a mean thing to do."

"I'm sorry for tricking you too," said Moon. "I hope that we can be friends again."

Sun perked up and nodded happily. "I would love that too," she said. The Wind and the Rain came out to join them, agreeing it was time for them all to make peace.

"Let's have some fun and create a giant storm," Lighting said to them all, flashing with excitement and electrifying the clouds. Wind howled fiercely, blowing with all his might, forming hurricanes and tornadoes down on earth. "Look how strong I am!" he said proudly to his friends in the sky. Cloud took a deep breath and released lots of rain, letting showers pour down and shimmer all around them. The friends were no longer fighting. They were happy to give each other their space in the sky and play games together again.

That is why the Sun is brighter than the Moon. Sun remains alone in the sky during the day, shining her brilliant light upon the earth. Moon shines her silvery glow at night but has her children for company. They are the beautiful stars twinkling brightly all around her.

Sirankomi the Hunter

(Mali)

Sirankomi the Hunter is a West African myth from Mali about the hunting methods of the Manden group of people. There are many versions of this story which try to explain how the Manden were such excellent hunters. This version is about a man who masters a secret, magical way of catching animals and what happens when he becomes too good at hunting.

A long time ago when the world was full of magical wonders, there lived a great hunter called Sirankomi. Even when Sirankomi was a small boy, with chubby cheeks and a single braid of hair, he showed early signs of becoming a skilled hunter. His family saw him creep up and surprise animals that were roaming around their home. He could track and hunt down any animal, never returning home empty-handed to his village.

"BOO," he cried, leaping out at lizards clinging upside down on a tree. The scaly creatures blinked their big eyes, wondering how such a small boy had spotted them, with their colours disappearing into the bark of a tree.

"Look what I found!" he shrieked proudly as he handed his mother a fluffy brown hare. He'd chased it down and grabbed hold of it in the forest. His mother wondered how her son was able to move so swiftly and quietly, without any animals knowing he was nearby. He still hadn't been trained, but it was clear to see he had talent.

Once Sirankomi was old enough to learn, his father taught him all the secrets of the bush. Sirankomi learned the ways to protect himself from the forest animals by mixing up potions of bitter herbs to drink. The dark syrupy liquid smelled of burnt ashes but gave him the power and strength to capture any prey. His father shared with him magical words to whisper into the night air to guard himself from the angry spirits of animals he had killed. And so it came to be that all the animals lived in fear of Sirankomi's shadow. Antelopes rarely heard his soft footsteps darting between the trees. Buffalo never saw his bamboo arrows flying at them through the air. Elephants were too slow to spot his traps.

With all of his natural talent along with the knowledge and alchemy passed down from his father, Sirankomi soon became a fierce hunter. By the time he was a young man, he was ready to go hunting by himself. He'd set off into the wooded forest wearing his *gris-gris*, a lucky charm pouch hanging around his neck, his leather hunting bag slung across his shoulder and iron weapons in his hands. Every day he returned with enough to feed the entire village. No animal felt safe and one by one they started to disappear from the forest, choosing to leave for new homes out of Sirankomi's reach. They feared that soon they would all die out and there would be none of their kind left to roam free.

One day, the lions called a meeting with all of the wild animals. They had decided that enough was enough; they all needed to put their differences aside and come up with a plan to get rid of Sirankomi. The lions passed their message to the leopards, who passed it on to the giraffes, who spread the word to the zebras, who told the monkeys and the buffalos, who carried it to the elephants, who shared it with the meerkats, who whispered it to the hyenas, who told everyone else. They all gathered far away from the village, past the empty fields and forest land, at the foot of a rugged mountain.

"I barely escaped from Sirankomi yesterday," began Hare. "He has been killing us nearly every day," she fumed.

"Soon we will be wiped out," said the meerkat. The other animals grunted and snarled in agreement.

"He knows what we will do before we even do it!" moaned Monkey. "I tried to trick him by swinging between the hanging vines, but he somehow got ahead of me." He held up his long arms to show how close he had been to Sirankomi.

"I circled back on him so that he would lose my trail, but he appeared out of nowhere," said

Cheetah, shaking his head in disbelief. Everyone was shocked – they knew Cheetah was the fastest animal among them.

"I called my friends to attack him, but he disappeared in the scuffle," huffed Buffalo.

"Our tricks do not work on Sirankomi the hunter. He is too clever," said Elephant. Lion stepped into the circle and growled, "Then we must learn what he knows and use it against him." Everyone went silent. They knew this had to be done, but no one wanted to get close to Sirankomi. They all feared for their lives.

"What shall we do?" asked Antelope. She held her head up high like a queen with her two horns pointing up for attention. She felt that they had complained enough and needed to make a decision. Hare jumped up and made a suggestion.

"One of us should visit him in disguise and learn his secrets. We can gain his trust and find out what his powers are." She stomped her feet on the ground, excited by her plan. Everyone liked this idea. But who would do it and what would be their disguise? they asked each other.

Hog smiled shyly and said, "I'll do it. I could disguise myself as a woman."

Hyena cackled out loud. "Do you really think you could look like a woman?"

"I'll do it," offered Giraffe. A few animals rolled their eyes and looked away. They knew that Giraffe was a bit clumsy, always tripping over her feet. Sirankomi would be sure to realize there was something funny about her.

"I'll do it," decided Buffalo. "I'll disguise myself as a man." Buffalo was strong and sensible. Everyone agreed that he was powerful enough to transform into a man to trick Sirankomi.

"I will become his friend and ask him to teach me the secret ways of the hunter. Once I know his powers, I will share them with you and we will catch *him*." Buffalo's words were greeted with lots of excitement. Anyone near the edge of the forest would have heard howling, cheering, screeching and roaring erupting from the animals.

It was twilight, that in-between time when the moon was rising, the sun's rays were dipping and the air grew potent with dark magic. Buffalo's enormous body could be seen rising out of the swamp. He stood beneath the trees with red mud dripping off his back and he danced a slow, shape-shifting dance. He moved his thick neck to the left and then to the right, with his white horns twisting and turning in the darkness. His heavy body became light, jumping and swaying from side to side. He grew long and lean, sprouting two muscly arms and legs. His face changed into a man's. His wide-open nostrils shrank in size. His jaw became chiselled and his eyes turned warm and friendly. He looked down and smiled, admiring his new shape. He touched his skin. *Ah, so soft and smooth*, he thought, *like polished ebony wood*. He walked out of the forest. Flecks of silvery light shone through the trees, revealing Buffalo now disguised as a tall young man.

The next day, Sirankomi sat outside sharpening his hunting knife when he saw a young man strolling up the path. Across his broad shoulders, he carried a huge stack of firewood, yet he walked as if they were tiny twigs.

"You must be very strong to carry all that wood so lightly," Sirankomi called out, impressed with the young man's strength. Buffalo smiled in reply and greeted Sirankomi with delight.

"I have been looking for you, Sirankomi! You are famous throughout all of the Manden villages for your fierce hunting," Buffalo said. "Please would you train me and teach me your ways? I will do anything to be your apprentice and master the ways of the hunter."

"I am pleased to meet you. It has been a long time since someone has asked for me." Sirankomi replied, feeling flattered. "Welcome to my home. First meet my parents and then tell me more about yourself and why you have come." Sirankomi smiled warmly and led him inside. He chatted with Buffalo over a meal of smoked fish and yams, made by his family. They sipped tea late into the night, whilst Buffalo praised Sirankomi's reputation and showed a great interest in his skills as a hunter.

"How do I know that you really are the great hunter Sirankomi? Tell me one of your secrets so that I can be sure."

Sirankomi hesitated. He knew that a hunter's secrets were very powerful. They were what kept him safe from harm.

Buffalo's dark eyes glowed warmly, and his friendly smile encouraged Sirankomi to trust him.

"Would you like to know about the leopard's secret hiding places? Or the hyena's swift movements? Or shall I tell you about the lions who dance when the moon is full?" asked Sirankomi, enjoying the chance to speak of his knowledge.

"No, every apprentice knows about those things." Buffalo waved his hand away and looked bored. "Tell me something that you have never shared with anyone else. Tell me, how do you stay alive when other men have been trampled by a herd of buffalos?"

"Ah, yes, those are very good questions. There are many times when I go into the bush and the animals are lying in wait for me. I have a way to escape them when danger is near." Sirankomi paused for a moment. He still was not sure if he could trust his new friend.

Before he could answer, his mother entered the room and offered their guest a bed for the night. "It is far too late for you to travel back to your own village; I will prepare a place for you to stay," she said kindly. Before she left the room, she whispered in Sirankomi's ear, "Be careful, my son. Do not reveal the secret of your strength to someone you have just met."

But Sirankomi saw Buffalo's young, eager face and felt at ease.

"Tell me more," urged Buffalo. "How do you

escape when you are cornered by animals in the bush?"

"I have mastered the secrets of transformations. I know how to shape-shift and change myself," said Sirankomi.

"Ahhh, I see." Buffalo breathed in the words and his eyes widened like two moons. "Tell me, what do you change into?" he asked.

"Sometimes an anthill."

"An anthill? What else?"

"Sometimes a tree stump."

"What else?"

"Then a patch of grass."

"What else?"

Before Sirankomi could reveal anything else, his mother appeared in the doorway.

"Sirankomi, your guest must be tired. Please be a good host and let him rest." She wanted to protect her son from giving away his secrets. She showed Buffalo to his room and everyone went to sleep.

The next day, Buffalo asked Sirankomi to go with him to his village. "I would like my family to meet Sirankomi, the hunter. Let me show you where I live."

Sirankomi accepted the invitation and prepared

to get his weapons and hunting bag, but Buffalo stopped him.

"You do not need to bring anything with you. It will not be a long journey. Come, let us go." He smiled broadly, flashing rows of white teeth.

Sirankomi shrugged and left all of his belongings behind. He walked empty-handed out of the village with Buffalo. They strolled across the rice fields, through the tall blades of grass. They walked all morning, whilst the sun hung like a ball of fire in the sky. "How much further to your village?" asked Sirankomi when they arrived at the edge of the forest.

"Oh, not much further, just on the other side of the forest," Buffalo said, pointing straight ahead. Sirankomi did not suspect anything at all. He was keen to meet Buffalo's friends, having passed such a pleasant evening with him. They walked through the forest where Sirankomi was used to hunting, crossing into a swampy marshland which was much further than he usually explored.

"Your village is not as near as I thought," said Sirankomi. He was starting to feel nervous about the distance they had travelled.

"Is the great hunter tired?" laughed Buffalo. "We

are very close," he lied. Finally, they came to a deserted area with very few shrubs. Only a giant baobab tree stood in the middle of a clearing.

"Where are we?" asked Sirankomi, looking around at the vast open land. There were no homes or people around them.

"We are here," Buffalo replied. He then let out a long, low whistle. It was a signal to his friends. Suddenly, all of the animals leaped out from their hiding places. Lion, Leopard and Cheetah sprang into the air with their claws ready to attack Sirankomi. Elephant charged towards him with her trunk stretched out. Zebra and Giraffe galloped at top speed, their legs kicking up dust as they ran. Buffalo had transformed back into his animal shape. He lowered his head, pointing his horns, ready to charge. Sirankomi recognized all of the animals he had ever hunted and knew they wanted revenge. He sprinted quickly behind the baobab tree before the animals could all pounce on him. Without anyone seeing, he changed into a small anthill at the foot of the tree.

"He has disappeared," shouted Hare, thumping her foot on the earth to warn them. The animals looked around and could see no sign of Sirankomi.

"He has changed himself into an anthill!" cried Buffalo. "Look around on the ground. Find him."

Hog used her long snout and tusks to search for an anthill around the tree.

"It's here!" she called out, and she began to dig up the earth. Sirankomi just had time to change again, this time into a stump, a little further from the tree.

"He is not hiding in the anthill," said Hog. They looked around again.

"He must have changed into a tree stump. Search again," called out Buffalo. The animals spread out and searched.

"He's here!" Elephant spotted a few small tree stumps and began to use his tusks to dig up the roots. He kicked them over with his wide feet but found nothing.

"Then he has changed again to a patch of green grass. Pull up the grass!" Buffalo instructed them all to move swiftly. With their heads bowed low, they set about ripping up grass patches wherever they saw it. Mud and hooves were flying everywhere. Sirankomi's powers were growing weaker. He was feeling very tired and had just enough strength for his last change. Without anyone noticing, he transformed into a small whirlwind of air, his last remaining secret. He spun around in tiny circles, dancing and floating away from the animals. They carried on ripping up the grass, furiously trying to find him. Buffalo had not found out about Sirankomi's last change. He could not offer any more help to the animals. The area around them was scattered with mud, roots and torn-up grasses. They finally gave up, exhausted from their searching.

"We may not have caught him this time, but now we know the secrets behind Sirankomi's hunting success, we can catch him if he ever comes back," said Buffalo. They disappeared back to their homes, after agreeing never to hunt each other again. In this way, the animals all became friends rather than enemies. Lion no longer hunted Hare, and Hyena no longer attacked Antelope. Everyone knew they would be safer if they looked out for one another.

Sirankomi the hunter escaped the animals that day and vowed never to share his secrets with any new visitors ever again.

Legends

The legends in this book tell of the first groups of people who lived in Africa and the Caribbean islands. They are stories rooted in history with real people and places that actually existed. Over time the stories have twisted and turned with the truth, like colourful yarn weaving itself into our imagination. Now you can decide where the truth ends and the story begins.

The Spear and the Bead

(UGANDA)

This is a legend about the origin of the Luo people of East Africa from the seventeenth century, who are found in southern Sudan, northern Uganda and Kenya. The story tells of a bitter feud between two brothers. An axe marks the spot in Uganda where the two brothers separated hundreds of years ago.

Back in the times when people moved freely across the plains of Africa, the Luo migrated south from Egypt. Travelling for weeks with their families and cattle, they finally settled in Pakwach, on the shores of the River Nile.

If you were around then, you would have seen the magnificent kingdom of wildlife, living alongside the Luo people. There were lions, leopards, antelopes and giraffes, all grazing and hunting together under the fierce gaze of the sun.

The Luo people were living together as one happy community, before a terrible family quarrel forced people to take sides.

The quarrel began with the death of the Luo's chief. He had led and protected the Luo people for many years, but when he grew old and died, it was time for the chiefdom to be passed to his eldest son, Lubongo.

A special coronation ceremony was held. All of the men and women gathered around in the main hut, dressed in their finest clothes. Terracotta-coloured togas and sashes made from the softest barkcloth were draped around their bodies.

Lubongo was dressed all in white, standing out from all of the other muted colours. He was handed a wooden ancestral spear. The long pole was etched with bright blue carvings with a sharp metal tip at the end. This ornate spear was a mark of his new leadership. He looked at it and felt such pride.

"I promise to guard the spear and hand it over to my first-born when the time comes," said Lubongo, bowing his head respectfully.

His younger brother, Gipir, was given a set of colourful royal beads which symbolized his nobility as the brother of the new chief. He felt happy for Lubongo and glad that he was also recognized in his new royal role.

With Lubongo as chief, the people lived harmoniously together for a short time. Their days were filled with herding cattle, planting vegetables and hunting wild animals. Until, one day, a blood-curdling scream pierced the air. Gipir rushed out of his hut and saw his wife running away from an elephant who had become separated from the herd. It was munching through their cowpeas, which was their main food for the season.

Lubongo was away hunting and Gipir was the only man left to defend their homes. Without any hesitation, he ran to the ceremonial hut where all the weapons were stored. He grabbed the first spear he laid his hand on and charged back outside towards the elephant.

"Get away, move away from our crops!" shouted Gipir. He was so worried that they would not have enough food left to harvest if he did not stop the elephant from eating it.

The elephant lifted its trunk high over its head and trumpeted loudly, terrifying everyone nearby. Women and children ran screaming into their huts. Black crows scattered from the trees and dark green turaco birds ran up and down their branches.

Gipir aimed his spear at the elephant and hurled it with all his might. The spear landed on the elephant's side and remained lodged. It cried out in agony. Then, fatally wounded, it limped away into the forest.

When Lubongo returned with the hunters several days later, they heard about Gipir's bravery and how he had saved their food from the elephant. To celebrate, everyone danced and sang in the shadows of the Miombo trees until late into the night.

It was not until the next day when Lubongo realized that the ancestral spear, which had been handed down to him from his father, making him chief, was missing. In his haste, Gipir had accidentally grabbed his brother's spear to attack the elephant.

"You had no right to use my spear. You must find it and return it to me," demanded Lubongo to his brother. He raged loudly to show that he was the chief, in charge.

"Lubongo, I'm sorry that I took your spear. I had to act quickly to save my wife and our crops," Gipir said. He hoped that his brother understood. But Lubongo was jealous of all of the attention Gipir was getting for being a hero.

"It is my job to protect our village. How can I do that, now you've taken my spear?" Lubongo said, furiously blinded by jealousy. Gipir was shocked. He couldn't believe his ears. Hadn't he saved the village?

"Brother, I will replace the spear with another, it can be easily done," Gipir offered, already turning away, but that made Lubongo even more angry.

"You are not taking this seriously. That spear is a symbol of my leadership. I will accept no other," he said.

"For your disrespect to me, you are banished from our village until you find my ancestral spear. Do not come back without it." Gipir couldn't believe his ears, but Lubongo was the chief and his word was final.

Gipir was deeply saddened by this and surprised that his brother would punish him so mercilessly in this way. They had always been so close. With a heavy heart, Gipir said goodbye to his wife and children, gathered as much food as he could carry, and set off to track the elephant.

He was an excellent hunter but would have to move fast to search the vast woodlands and valleys. The elephant already had a head start of several days. He could now be anywhere.

Gipir immediately spotted drops of blood from the elephant's wounds and crushed bushes where it had staggered away. But after a few days, the clues disappeared. As hard as he tried, using all the hunting tricks he knew, Gipir could see no other signs of where the elephant had gone.

As days turned to weeks, Gipir started to give up. His food was almost gone and he was growing weaker every day, with very little water left. He saw spotted hyenas and black-maned lions circling around him from afar and began to be afraid he would not survive his hunt. He slowly made his way through the dry acacia woodland, cursing his brother for not forgiving him and sending him away. He finally found shade and sat down under a tall candelabra tree.

I'm going to die here, thought Gipir sadly. *I will never see my wife and children again. If only I could find some water, perhaps I could regain my strength and return to see my family.*

He felt weak and his eyes began to close. Just as they fluttered shut, he saw an old woman appearing in the distance. He blinked. Was she really there? She was dressed in a long black gown with a scarf covering her head. She walked briskly towards him. He blinked again. Yes, she was still there. She carried a large flask in her hands. Water! Gipir felt a flicker of hope. She was not an illusion. The old woman came close to his face and stared at him. "Drink this," she said, and put her flask to his lips. Gipir sipped slowly. Cool water trickled down his face, waking him up and reviving him a little. He felt such relief. She was really here and now he was saved!

"Can you walk?" she asked, helping him to sit up. "My home is not far; come with me." She helped him to his feet and led him slowly towards her home in the grassy swampland. He was thankful but too tired to speak. He lay down and drifted to sleep. It was morning before he woke up to the smell of bitter herbs. The old woman had been mixing up an ancient remedy to nurse him back to good health. "Drink this," she said firmly, handing him a warm cup. Gipir wrinkled up his nose. It smelled horrible, but he drank it and fell back to sleep.

Over the next few days, Gipir gradually regained his strength. But every night he cried himself to sleep because he missed his family so much. One evening as they sat around a fire eating some stew, she asked him, "Where were you going when I found you? There is nothing but swamps around here."

Gipir's face became shadowed with sadness. With a heavy heart he spoke. "I was tracking an elephant and became lost. I wounded it with my brother's ancestral spear. He has banished me until I find his spear, which disappeared with the elephant."

To his surprise, Gipir saw that the old woman was smiling. "I can help you," she said.

"How?" he asked in wonder.

"Because I have watched the elephants for years. I have seen where the elephants go to live and where they go to die. That is where your spear will be," she said.

Gipir thanked the old woman for her wisdom and listened carefully as she gave him instructions on where to find the resting place of the elephants.

"Follow the curve of the river and walk until the new moon ends and you see its silver crescent in the sky. By then you will be out of the desert and have reached the valley of giraffes. Walk until the trees begin to part and the ground starts to crack, and there you will see where the elephants go to die."

The next day, Gipir set off, thanking the old woman for her help and for nursing him back to full health. He followed the curve of the river until the sun lay in the east. He walked for many days and nights until he saw a crescent-shaped moon cradled in the night sky. Just as the old woman had told him, he came across a field of giraffes. They stood still in straight lines, like tall statues. With their long regal necks stretching up, towards the sky. It was a wondrous sight but Gipir could only think of his task.

I must be close to where the elephants go to die, thought Gipir, hope rising in his chest. Surely if he found the spear there, he would finally be able to return home to his family. His steps gathered pace until he found himself running through the forest. Gradually the trees began to clear and sunlight streamed through as he left the forest. The earth beneath him was dry and starting to crack in places. He entered a rugged valley, flanked by mountains. Suddenly, he heard a long, sharp whistle ringing out above him. Gipir looked up and saw an eagle swooping and rocking from side to side, its talons stretched out and ready to pounce. He darted to the side of a giant rock, breathing heavily, and waited for it to pass.

He was tired and wanted to stop for a rest but knew he had to get there before dark. He pushed himself on, noticing that he was coming to the end of the valley. The mountains were clearing and the ground beneath him felt dusty and cracked. He was so excited to see many spears scattered all around. Surely one of these belonged to his brother. He peered closely and saw some rusty and worn, others tipped with blood and many broken and split.

Gipir gazed at the many weapons from hunters like himself, used to attack and kill elephants. He was so shocked at how many there were. He stepped over dome-shaped skulls and walked through giant ribcages that once had belonged to elephants. It was an incredible sight. And there, amid the bones and the spears, a bright blue colour caught his eye. He reached down and found his brother's magnificent spear, with carvings along the pole. Gipir gave a huge shout of joy, at last he could return home and see his family! He immediately turned on his heel and retraced his steps, making his way back to the old woman's hut to thank her one last time.

"Thank you for saving my life. Now I can go back to my family," said Gipir.

She smiled at his delight, and gave him a gift in return for his help in mending her house – a bowl full of brightly coloured beads. "Take these precious beads to add to your collection. Remember that you too are a noble leader, and one who has defended your village from elephants!"

Gipir began his weary journey home, holding the precious beads the old woman had given him in one hand, and the spear of his brother in the other.

When he finally reached his village, he fell to his knees and kissed the earth. At last he was home!

Lubongo saw Gipir and instantly rushed over to greet him. "Welcome back, brother! It has been far too long," he cried out in happiness. They hugged each other tightly, as if no time had passed between them. Gipir handed over the ancestral spear which had caused so much strife, but Lubongo was no longer interested in that, he was so overjoyed to have his brother back. Instead he called out to everyone, "Gipir has returned, my brother has returned!" Family, friends and neighbours gathered around to celebrate and cheer.

Gipir's wife was returning from the fields when she heard all the uproar from the villagers. She strained her eyes, trying to see what was causing such a commotion. When she saw Gipir emerging from the crowd, she gasped out loud in shock, dropping her basket of seeds all over the ground. "Is that you, Gipir?" she yelled out in surprise, but her feet were already running towards him. She had dreamed of this moment every day since he left and now she felt elated that he was finally here. They hugged each other warmly, happy to be reunited at last.

Once they were alone, Gipir gave his wife the exquisite beads he'd received from the old woman.

She gazed at the mix of colours which bounced off each one, giving them a striking glow. "These beads are beautiful and so rare," she said, accepting them from him with pride. The following day, she invited some of the women to come round to admire her new collection of beads.

Gipir's wife placed the colourful beads in small bowls, displaying them proudly for all to see. But while Lubongo's wife looked at the beads with the other women, her baby girl crawled over and picked up one of the orange beads. No one saw her put the oval-shaped bead into her mouth until it was too late. She swallowed it and began to cry. Her mother firmly tapped her back and tried to get the child to cough the bead up, but that did not work. The bead was gone.

That evening, Gipir's wife explained to him what had happened during the day with Lubongo's baby daughter, laughing at the accident and exclaiming how lucky they were that the child wasn't injured. But Gipir didn't laugh at the near calamity. He was furious. Completely enraged, he marched straight over to his brother's house and demanded that his brother return the bead at once. Lubongo waved his brother away and said, "The bead will pass through my daughter in a day or so and then you shall have it back."

When two days had passed and the bead still had not come out in the baby's stool, Lubongo made another suggestion.

"Do not worry, Gipir, I can give you another bead to replace what has been lost," he offered without much concern, not realizing how angry his brother was.

"I want my bead, the same bead that your daughter has swallowed. No other will do," ordered Gipir, his eyes bulging with rage as he faced his brother.

Lubongo tried to calm him down, realising that this row was not just about the bead. Gipir still felt furious at the way he had been treated by his brother, being banished from his home and family to find the spear.

"Give me a few more days, brother," appealed Lubongo, trying now to calm Gipir down. "It will show up or we will come to another agreement," he said. This time Lubongo's tone was conciliatory and he invited Gipir to dine with him the next evening in an effort to make peace. The two brothers sat outside, eating their warm *matoke* of steamed green bananas, after a filling meal of roasted meats.

Villagers walked past and saw the two brothers talking together until late into the evening, when the spotted owls could be heard whistling in the distance. People thought that their disagreement would blow over and smiled to see the two together. But at first light, when the cuckoo birds woke everyone with their chattering call, Gipir stood outside of Lubongo's hut and shouted, "Brother! You have had several days to return my precious bead and still you have brought me nothing. Now you must cut open your child and fetch me my bead." His eyes darkened with the memory of nearly dying alone in the desert without seeing his own children again.

Lubongo could not believe what he was hearing. Surely Gipir couldn't mean for him to cut his own daughter open, all for a little bead? He offered again to replace the bead with other objects, but Gipir was blind with bitterness and wanted revenge.

Pleading for Gipir to see sense, Lubongo took their quarrel to the council of elders who advised the chief, asking for their help.

The elders met in a rectangular hut, reserved for rituals and meetings. They listened to both sides of the story and warned each brother of the consequences of their actions.

"*Okufa nkovu etawona.* Death is a scar that never heals," said one of the elders, hoping that they would forgive each other. But Gipir did not want to listen. He wanted justice. He turned to the elders and said, "My brother has set the rules and he must live by them too," he said, through gritted teeth. His heart had turned to ice and nothing would melt it. Lubongo stood rigid and tall, like an unbending tree. He was too proud to beg for mercy. The elders listened in sorrow, wishing there was something they could say to change Gipir's mind. After many hours of debating, they came to their conclusion and brought the argument to an end.

"We have asked you both to make peace with the past and forget your earlier quarrel. But as Gipir accepted Lubongo's price for losing his royal spear, now Lubongo, you must accept Gipir's price for losing his royal bead," the elders announced to them both. As soon as the judgement was made, Lubongo's wife cried out in anguish, but she knew that nothing could be done to save their daughter. She would be killed to return the royal bead.

From that day on, both Gipir and Lubongo could not bear to live with each other, one still furious over the way he had been banished, the other heartbroken over the death of his child. They agreed the only way to survive was to go their separate ways, never to see each other again. They took an axe and plunged it into the earth where they stood, to divide up the land between them. And that is how the Luo people were split into two.

Gipir moved his family and a few of his people west of the River Nile to set up his land. They became the Alur people in Uganda.

Lubongo and his family migrated east of the Nile and settled in Kenya.

The axe is believed to be buried in the area we now call Wang-Lei on the shores of the River Nile. If you go there today, you will find this spot a few metres from Pakwach bridge. It remains as a reminder of the ancestry of the Luo people, and a reminder for everyone to be kind to one another.

The Legend of Victoria Amazonica

(Guyana)

This legend originates from the indigenous people of Guyana who lived nearly three thousand years ago. It is a story about a young Carib girl and her quest to reach the moon and the stars.

In a time before me and a time before you, the Caribs were also known as the water people. They lived in villages scattered around the rivers, creeks and streams of Guyana.

Our story begins near the Amazon River, the second-longest river in the world. It snakes and bends across South America, and it is here the Caribs carved canoes from the trunks of palm trees, twisted leaves to weave baskets and feasted on the flesh of its fruits.

Every night, the eldest girls would gather under a tree to share stories of times and traditions gone by. Their long dark hair hung like cloaks around their backs and their skin shone like cinnamon trees in the darkness. The youngest of their group was called Aiyana, and she would look up at the sky, letting the stories of gods and goddess carry her away, dreaming of the stars above. After all, it was well-known among her people that if you could touch the thing you dreamed of, you would become just as beautiful and powerful as the object you touched.

"Oh, how I wish we could touch the moon and the stars," said Aiyana. The magical stories had enchanted her so much that she desperately wanted to seek out the beauty and power held within the night sky.

The next evening, the full face of the beautiful moon could be seen. Aiyana and her friends were sitting underneath a cannonball tree, and Aiyana was dreaming of climbing into the sky as usual. She could smell the cannonball tree's sweet-scented flowers spiralling around the trunk. She reached out and plucked one of the cannonballs of fruit that hung swollen and heavy in between the flowers. Then an idea came to her.

"If I climb to the top of this tree, I will be closer to the sky. I can reach out and touch the moon or the stars."

Without waiting for her friends, she climbed fearlessly up the trunk of the tree, stepping on the cannonballs and pulling on its vines. She crawled between the cramped spaces of its branches and reached out her hand to touch the moon in the sky. She still could not reach it, but she would not give up.

The following evening, Aiyana came up with another idea. She turned to her friends, who sat gathered around her.

"Follow me up to the highest mountain peak,"

she said. "From there we can gaze in wonder at the night sky and reach out to finally grasp the moon."

With the sky lit up by the stars above, Aiyana led her friends to the nearest mountain. They walked down into valleys, through forests and clambered over rocks until they finally reached the peak of the mountain. There, they stretched their arms out to the night sky, only to be disappointed again when they could not touch the moon.

The following night, when they had finished telling their stories and songs, Aiyana took one of their dugout canoes and sailed down the river. The thought of touching the moon consumed her and she couldn't give up on her dream. The air was damp with heat and she lowered her hands into the river while floating aimlessly along. Just ahead of her, she noticed the reflection of the moon, luminous and rippling in the water.

At last, she thought. *I can reach out and touch it.* She beamed with happiness at the thought of finally reaching the moon. Without a moment's hesitation, she dived into the water, breaking through the reflection of the moon. She pushed herself down and sank deep into the river, twisting through giant reeds and moss, searching for the moon she thought she saw in the water. But she couldn't find it. Soon the water became still and there was no sign of Aiyana. She was trapped under the water in the reeds and the moss, struggling for breath.

The water goddess Atabey looked down from her place in the sky and was saddened to see the young girl struggling. As the supreme goddess of rivers, lakes and seas, Atabey had the power to save Aiyana. So the goddess sent a stream of glowing green light that swirled beneath the water, changing the current and turning the tide.

But the gods' gifts are never straightforward, and instead of coming up to the surface, Aiyana's body slowly transformed into a large flower with layers of petals that cradled each other – a dark green, graceful water lily. As the sun warmed the earth, each petal gently changed colour from white to pink as it blossomed over the day.

And so the story goes that Aiyana's dream came true and she gained the beauty she wanted, but not the way she wished. She is known to this very day as the Victoria Amazonica – the largest water lily in the world with the most intoxicating scent. If you travel to Guyana, you can see these giant water lilies fanned out in all their glory, floating on the surface of the rivers and changing their colours throughout the day.

The Bite of the Loup Garou

(HAITI)

Loup Garous or Lagahoos have been spotted around the Caribbean, where it is believed that certain people transform into these monstrous beasts (also known as werewolves) when the moon is full. This legend tells of a wealthy man in the community who is suspected of being a Loup Garou.

Mr Saint-Clair was known as the meanest man in the town of Kenscoff. He owned most of the farmland up in the green mountains. Many people in the town worked long hours for him every day, toiling in his fields, tending his crops. They were rarely allowed to have a day off. If they turned up late or were sick, Mr Saint-Clair would pay them less. If anyone owed him money, he would scare them into paying more by threatening to take away their land. When the farm crops did not grow well, he would take the cost out of their pay. No one liked working for Mr Saint-Clair, but they had very little choice. He owned nearly everything and there was no other work to be had.

Mr Saint-Clair was quite a flashy man who liked to be seen and heard around town. He strutted about in a white linen suit and blue hat, like a royal flycatcher bird with feathers fanned out above its head. He had round, glassy eyes that swallowed you up whole if you stared into them. One day, he dressed in his best suit, placed his blue hat on his head, and left his house to visit a man called Baptiste and his wife Camille. They lived on a small farm in one of the low valleys that Mr Saint-Clair really wanted. He had offered them lots of money to buy their farm, but they always refused to sell. Their land was bursting with colourful plants and lively sounds from all of the animals. Yellow trumpet flowers hung like giant bells from their stalks. String beans, sweet peas and vegetables of all shapes and sizes grew in long rows and wide circles in their fields.

Mr Saint-Clair breezed up the path and found Baptiste digging up potatoes next to their house.

"Hello, Baptiste, how are you?" He smiled and tipped his blue hat to greet him. Baptiste nodded and carried on digging, barely looking up. Mr Saint-Clair continued. "I heard that some of your animals have been sick lately. Perhaps you will be willing to sell them to me for half the price I first offered?" He pushed his round face closer to Baptiste, who continued to dig.

"We don't need your help, thank you. The animals are just a bit tired," Baptiste replied, wondering how Mr Saint-Clair had found out about the sick animals. Both he and his wife had been careful not to tell many people so that the news would not get to Mr Saint-Clair. A few nights before, when the moon was at its fullest in the sky, their pigs had gone wild in their pen for three whole nights.

Baptiste and Camille heard them grunting and snorting loudly, kicking the fences down. They could not understand what had set them off. Since then, the pigs had looked pale and weak and were eating very little.

"I've heard that a sickness is spreading across the farms," said Mr Saint-Clair, shaking his head in fake concern. "Mr Claude's animals became sick and very weak, so he asked me to buy them from him." Mr Saint-Clair grinned, showing rows of brilliant white teeth. Baptiste stopped digging and looked up in surprise. This was troubling news indeed. If their neighbour, Mr Claude, had sold his animals, how long would it be before they had to sell theirs too?

"You should consider my offer whilst your animals are still worth something. I might not be so generous next time," said Mr Saint-Clair a bit more forcefully.

"I don't care what you offer This is our land and I will never sell to you," said Baptiste, raising his voice. He stood up straight and glared into Mr Saint-Clair's glassy eyes.

"I'll return in a few days and see if you've changed your mind." He smiled a mysterious smile, as if he knew something that Baptiste didn't, tipped his hat and walked away.

Later that evening, over a pot of spicy joumou soup with beef and pumpkin, Baptiste and his wife came up with a plan.

"Let us keep watch every night until we find out what is upsetting our animals," they said to each other. They agreed to take turns, with Baptiste starting first that very night. He nestled down in the barn behind some hay, where their donkeys slept. As the darkness settled in, Baptiste twitched nervously at every terrifying sound he heard. Owls screeched in the distance, rats scuttled across the roof and frogs whistled long and low in the trees. He imagined light-footed creatures charging across his fields, preparing to gobble him and all their farm animals up.

Stop those silly thoughts, Baptiste. He spoke sternly to himself, trying to get rid of his imaginary monsters. His eyes stung with tiredness and without realizing it, he soon drifted off to sleep on the floor.

A little later, the sound of a creaking door woke him up. Someone had come into the barn. Baptiste sat up and let his eyes adjust to the darkness, trying to see what was shuffling across the floor. Suddenly, the donkeys let out a loud *hee-haw*. Baptiste rushed over and shone a torch on the donkeys. He cried out in fright, seeing they'd been bitten on their legs by what looked like a hairy beast, the size of a large dog. Baptiste caught sight of its red eyes, which sat like two pools of blood in its hairy face. The beast stood up straight on two legs, growled and ran out of the barn. The donkeys kicked their back legs against the wall, yelping and braying loudly. They broke down their fence and galloped like a herd of horses out of the barn, followed by the pigs and other animals. Camille heard the commotion from the house and appeared in the doorway with a lamp.

"Baptiste! What's happening?" she called out frantically, and then saw him shivering in a corner of the barn. Terror dripped from his face into a puddle of sweat.

"I saw something terrible, Camille. A beast." His voice quivered and then he stopped, too scared to say any more. She grabbed his hands and dragged him with her.

"Come, Baptiste, we need to stop the animals from getting away," she said, tugging him along. They walked up high into the mountains, following the sound of the braying donkeys. Giant tree ferns loomed on either side. Their branches stretched out towards them as if screaming in horror. The air was cool with the smell of damp leaves from the rain which fell gently around them.

"Camille, I'm scared." Baptiste was shaking and looking all around them. He did not want to walk any further. He could not get the image of the hairy beast out of his mind, but his wife was determined to find their animals. The moon shone through the trees, casting silvery shadows on the ground. It was the twilight hour. That in-between time which does not belong to the day or the night. The animal sounds grew closer and closer. Snorting, neighing, barking, growling all clashed together in a rowdy mess. Baptiste and Camille turned a corner and saw an unbelievable sight. Pigs were leaping through the air. Goats were jumping, donkeys were twirling and chickens were rolling around on the ground. In the middle of all this commotion sat the hairy beast which Baptiste had seen in their barn. Its face was pointing up into the night sky as it howled into the blackness. Baptiste turned to run but Camille stopped him. She reached down to the ground and grabbed a handful of dirt.

"Rub this on your forehead," she whispered. He did as he was told and then she called out to their animals, "Get back to your homes! Quick now, shoo!"

All of the animals suddenly stopped leaping about and scurried back to their pens on the farm. The hairy beast took one look at Camille and ran away into the woods. Baptiste stared at his wife in awe and wonder. "How did you know what to do?" he asked in a trembling voice. Camille told him how she had heard stories from her grandmother Fabienne about bewitched animals and shape-shifters.

"At the end of the stories, she told me that if I ever come across any hairless pigs or goats leaping about in the magical twilight hours, I must gather earth from the ground and rub it on to my forehead." Baptiste frowned, still not quite understanding why. Camille put on her grandmother's voice and wagged her finger just as she had. "The earth will protect you and the shape-shifters will never trouble you, my child."

Baptiste sighed in relief. He too had heard the stories about shape-shifting animals but he always believed they were just made-up stories. Now he wasn't so sure. The pair walked slowly back to their farm, leading the animals behind them and wondering if the nightmare was over. They needed to be sure that the beast would not come back and harm their animals. The following day, they went to see Jean-Paul, an elder in the town, to ask for advice. His hair was crystal white with all his years of wisdom and he was known to carry all of the traditions and stories from generations gone by. If anyone knew how to help them, it would be him. They found Jean-Paul in his garden, resting in a hammock beneath his favourite orange trees. His eyes were closed, but he heard their footsteps approaching and sat up to greet them warmly.

"Camille and Baptiste! What can I help you with today?" His grey eyes twinkled with the excitement of having visitors. "Let me offer you some coconut water." He welcomed them into his garden and they sat in the shade discussing the night's events. Jean-Paul listened carefully to their story and shook his head sadly.

"You have been visited by a Loup Garou," he said gravely. "A werewolf that comes and bites your animals, leading them into a wild dance at night. That is why they are so weak and sick during the day."

"I knew it!" said Camille, and told Jean-Paul how they had gotten rid of the Loup Garou. He praised them for their bravery but said in a sombre voice, "It is not over yet."

"What can we do to get rid of it?" Baptiste asked fearfully. "If we can't protect our animals, we won't be able to feed ourselves and Mr Saint-Clair will buy up our land."

"On the next full moon, you must lie in wait with a strong rope and net. When you see it appear you must trap it and hold it in place." Jean-Paul explained that this was the only way.

Baptiste gasped. "Why do we need to catch the beast? Surely it would be better to kill it?" he asked.

"It is not easy to get rid of a Loup Garou, but if you trap it until sunrise, it will change back into a human and the curse will be lifted for ever," Jean-Paul told them. "You will be free of it. There is no other way." Baptiste and Camille looked at each other but nodded grimly, knowing that they would have to face the Loup Garou again.

When they reached home once more, Mr Saint-Clair was waiting for them. He'd somehow found out about their animals going wild the night before and wanted to offer his help. He held out a small bag of golden coins.

"Why don't you sell me your farm with these troublesome animals? I can take them off your hands right now." His glassy eyes were swimming with greed as he waved the bag in front of them, trying not to look around at the lush land that he wanted for himself.

Baptiste shook his head and refused the money, asking Mr Saint-Clair to leave. *How does he know of our troubles?* Baptiste thought. *We have only told Jean-Paul and there is no way that news could have travelled so fast.*

When the full moon came around, Baptiste and Camille were ready to trap the Loup Garou. They secretly hoped that it would never come back, but just in case Jean-Claude was right, they both hid behind their barn that night. The animals were locked up and resting inside. The wind blew stronger through the night air, carrying sweet smells of cinnamon from the mountains. No one heard the Loup Garou treading softly in the darkness. No one saw its long teeth glinting in the moonlight. The hairy beast stalked past the barn and towards the chicken coup. It clawed through the ground, trying to dig its way in. The chickens started to fuss and fret, clucking loudly. Baptiste realized something must be wrong. He signalled to his wife and together they tiptoed in the darkness to where the sounds were coming from. They saw the great big Loup Garou and lifted their hands together to throw a large net over it. They pulled the end of the net tightly and tied it with their rope. The hairy beast realized it was trapped and it tried to wriggle free, growling and barking furiously. Baptiste and Camille held on together and watched with wide-open eyes as the werewolf shape-shifted. It transformed into a hairless pig and then a goat and then a cat. Each change found it hissing and snarling, desperately trying to wriggle free. Camille tied the end of the rope around the trunk of a tree and there the pair sat waiting for the sun to rise. It seemed to take hours as the transformations continued until finally the dark sky faded away, leaving sunlight to creep in.

"Look, Camille, look at it changing!" Baptiste shook his wife in disbelief as they saw the Loup Garou transform into its true self. Lying in the net, beside the tree on their farmland, was Mr Saint-Clair.

"*You* are the wild beast that has been terrorizing our animals!" Baptiste called out in surprise. Camille stood gaping in disbelief.

"Please forgive me, I couldn't help myself," Mr Saint-Clair begged, cowering in the net.

"You wicked, greedy man!" Camille had finally found her voice and she was furious. "We ought to take you through the village and show everyone that you were the Loup Garou," she said.

"No, no. Please don't do that. If you let me go, I promise never to return to Kenscoff town. I'll leave you all in peace," he muttered weakly.

Baptiste and Camille hesitated. They wanted to make sure that everyone would be free from his grasping hands.

"Before you leave, return all of the farms back to the farmers, so that they can own their own animals and land. If you do that, we will keep your secret," Baptiste said firmly, locking eyes with Mr Saint-Clair to make sure he understood.

"Yes, of course. Anything you want, just please set me free," he pleaded, with tears streaming down his face.

Baptiste paused, wondering if they could really trust him. Camille grabbed the rope from her husband and pulled it tightly. Mr Saint-Clair shrieked, worried that they would leave him there in the forest.

"We know all about you now, Mr Saint-Clair. If you ever come back, we will tell all the villagers about you." Her words were sharp, making him flinch at the thought of being shamed. He nodded quickly in reply. Feeling satisfied that he understood, Camille untied the rope, letting Mr Saint-Clair go.

Later that day, just as he'd agreed, Mr Saint-Clair handed over documents to all of the farmers, proving that they were the true owners of their land. Everyone was surprised at his sudden generosity, but nobody questioned it in case he changed his mind.

Mr Saint-Clair gathered what was left of his riches, all the wealth he had stored and set off for another island to start a new life. Some say they still hear him howling in the forest when the moon is full, but Baptiste and Camille never heard from him again and lived happily on their farm for the rest of their days.

The Legend of the Hummingbird

(PUERTO RICO)

This is a well-known legend from Puerto Rico about the indigenous people on the island. It tells the story of two star-crossed lovers whose families tried to keep them apart.

Many, many years ago, the Taino people settled deep in the mountains of a tropical rainforest. Their chief had led them across rolling hills and cavernous rocks to find a new home away from the Caribs who were their enemies.

Alida was the eldest daughter of the Taino chief. When the men were out fishing and the women were weaving, she would sometimes leave the village and visit her favourite place. It was a tranquil pool of bright blue water that flowed from a tumbling waterfall. The only way to reach it was to hike through the forest towards the cliff edge and climb down a steep slope of rocks. There, she would relax and pick fruit from the trees.

On one of these days, Alida expected to be alone as usual. She dived into the pool and swam among the fishes, enjoying her freedom and solitude. Afterwards, she sat drying off on the rocks, when she suddenly heard a branch crack. Alida quickly grabbed her bow and arrow. In the bushes stood a young man.

"Who are you and what do you want?" she asked, aiming her arrow directly at his heart. She did not recognize him. His tight curly hair was covered with a headband of feathers that fanned out above his head, worn differently from her villagers.

"My name is Taroo," said the young man. "I come here to pick the sweetest rose apples." He pointed at the tree, hoping that she would understand his language, but she did not. She moved closer with her bow. "I have seen you here before," he said quickly. "I kept wishing I would see you again so that I could speak to you." He lowered his eyes and blushed a little. Alida relaxed; she recognized some of his words and let down her bow.

"I am Alida, eldest daughter of our *cacique*, chief," she said proudly in her language. He nodded to show that he understood.

She discovered that Taroo belonged to the Carib group of people who were at war with her family. The Caribs had moved on many months ago to another land, but Taroo had been accidentally left behind.

"You live here alone in the forest without your family?" she asked, amazed by his bravery. They spent hours together, laughing and drawing pictures in the sand to explain each other's words, before Alida had to return to her family.

Alida and Taroo continued to secretly meet at the waterfall pool every time Alida could get away from her chores. They swam, picked fruits and kept each other company. Even though they spoke different languages, they had fun trying to understand each other by pointing and doing actions.

Taroo taught Alida how to say words in his Carib language, like *weju* for sun and *nuno* for moon. She taught him the words from her Taino language, like *iro* for man and *inaru* for woman. It was not long before they had fallen in love and were meeting nearly every day.

Alida's absences from the village didn't go unnoticed. One of her cousins decided to follow her one morning to see where she was going. He saw her run swiftly through the forest towards the cliff edge. He peered over the rocks into the pool below and saw Alida rush into the arms of Taroo. They embraced, believing that they were alone. Alida's cousin felt rage rising up in his chest when he saw them together. He believed that Taroo was their enemy and would cause them harm. He ran swiftly back to Alida's father to tell him what she was doing.

"I followed Alida today because she has been sneaking off alone and refusing to tell me where she is going," he said to the chief.

"What do you mean? You have been spying on my daughter?" bellowed the chief, not liking where the conversation was going. Her cousin shrank back a little and then blurted out his news. "She has been secretly meeting with a Carib warrior. Alone! I saw them together." His words flew through the air like poison arrows, stabbing her father's heart. The chief felt alarmed at what he was hearing. He did not want to believe it. How could his daughter deceive them like this by meeting with an enemy? He dismissed her cousin angrily and summoned a guard to fetch Alida to his hut.

"Is it true that you have been meeting with a Carib warrior?" her father asked her, still hoping that it would not be true.

She lowered her eyes and felt her face burn with shame. The Caribs had raided their villages many times in the past, torturing the men and capturing the women. She knew her love for Taroo would be considered the ultimate betrayal by her people.

"You know they are our enemies!" said her father, shaking with anger. "He could be planning to raid our village with others," he raged, his voice thundering into the skies.

"No, Father! Taroo is not like the others. He is here alone," she cried, immediately regretting her words.

"Alone? Even better. We can capture him easily

before he warns the rest of his people." Her father's face contorted with thoughts of revenge on the young man. He pushed Alida aside and signalled his guard to bring weapons.

"Please, Father. I'm begging you. Do not kill Taroo." She blocked his way and fell to her knees, grabbing his hand as she once used to. "I promise never to see him again, if only you spare his life." He looked down at his daughter, her tears soaking his hand, and his heart softened. He did not want to hurt her but he was torn. He needed to protect the village from this interloper.

"I should hunt him down like a bear," he said to himself, knowing what would be expected of him as the chief. The guards returned carrying spears and clubs, ready to track down Taroo. They waited in silence for the chief's instructions. Alida squeezed her father's hand again, hoping that he would show mercy. He looked at his guards, who were waiting eagerly, and then looked at his daughter, who was trembling with fear. Finally he said to the guards, "Put down your weapons. We will not hunt him today." He turned to Alida and continued, "But you are banned from seeing him ever again! If Taroo sets foot in our village, we will kill him," he promised, helping her rise to her feet. She sighed with relief and hugged her father tightly, thanking him for being merciful.

The next day, Alida was ordered to remain in the village with the other women. She spent her time weaving hammocks and carving wooden statues of their gods, *zemis*. She missed Taroo desperately and prayed that he would not come looking for her.

Taroo returned to the pool every day to wait for Alida, but she didn't come. After a few days, desperate to see her, he went to the outskirts of her village, hoping to catch a glimpse of her entering or leaving. He climbed up the trunk of a silk-cotton tree that towered over her village like a giant beanstalk. He hid within the knotted branches and kept watch all day but saw no glimpse of his love. Under the cloak of darkness, when he thought it was safe to leave, Taroo climbed down from the tree and returned to his home. But one of the Taino guards spotted him leaving and reported it to the chief.

"I saw someone I did not recognize, running away from our village last night," said the guard in the chief's hut.

"Was it the Carib warrior? Where did he go?"

asked Alida's father, already grabbing his spear and preparing to rouse his guards.

"I cannot be sure. It was dark and I lost sight of him," he said. He hung his head low and waited to be issued a punishment.

"If it was him, he was probably looking for my daughter. Go back to your post and keep a closer watch," ordered the chief. He paced up and down inside his hut, feeling anxious that she might be planning to run away with Taroo. How could he stop this from happening? His mind raced with ideas of how to keep them apart. "I could secretly have him killed," he said to himself, but soon dismissed that idea, knowing Alida would never forgive him. "I could put more guards around our village," but that idea could not go on for ever. At last the perfect idea came to him. "I will arrange for her to be married to someone else." This idea sat well with him. It would happen one day, so why not now? As soon as the chief decided, a suitable man from a nearby village was chosen. Alida was brought to the ceremonial hut to be told the news by her mother and aunties. They surrounded her with smiles and cheering, believing this to be wonderful news.

"You are to be married to Kaonati from the next village," they sang at the top of their voices, clapping and dancing joyously around her. Alida stood still in the middle of them, stunned into silence. This was the last thing she wanted to happen. Her heart still belonged to Taroo. Once she was alone with her father, she told him of her feelings.

"Father, I respect your decision, but I cannot marry Kaonati. I do not love him," she said firmly, with defiance in her eyes. But her father's mind was made up and nothing would sway him, not even his daughter's tears.

"You will learn to love him," he said coldly, and turned away from her, refusing to hear any more excuses.

The wedding preparations began the next day, with the village plaza decorated with plaited leaves and sweet-smelling flowers. Ceremonial dancers began the celebration, dancing to the beat of their drums. Alida was fussed over by many of the women. They painted her face in bright colours, whilst hanging gold necklaces and strings of shells around her neck. She stood in a daze, whilst their voices hummed around her.

"Ah, you look so beautiful," said one auntie.

"What a lucky girl you are," said another.

"How happy you must be," they all agreed before leaving her to finish getting ready.

Once she was alone, Alida fell to her knees and cried out to their gods for help.

"Please save me from this marriage. Rescue me now, I beg you." She held up her hands, wishing that she could be taken away from there.

As soon as her grief-stricken words were uttered, Yocahu, son of the goddess Atabey, took pity upon Alida. He looked down from the sky and whispered words of comfort into Alida's ears.

"Dry your eyes, there is nothing to fear. I will change you into a flower and take you from here." The god's words soothed Alida and gave her hope. *I would rather join the gods in nature and become part of the beautiful landscape than live without Taroo,* she thought desperately. With a flurry of golden light from the stars up above, Yocahu transformed her into a bright red flower. He gently carried her out of the village and placed her safely on the wooded slopes of the forest.

As the weeks passed without Alida's return, Taroo gave up hope of ever seeing her again. Filled with sadness, he too cried out to Yocahu, begging for answers. The god spoke from his place in the sky and explained what had happened.

"Where can I find this red flower?" cried Taroo in despair. "I cannot live without Alida."

Yocahu could not point out where Alida was because the hillside was filled with so many red flowers. All he could do to ease Taroo's pain was to transform him into a tiny multicoloured bird.

"Go and find your love, little bird," said Yocahu. "She is on the mountainside."

Taroo flew away, with his wings vibrating very fast. The next day, two villagers were walking in the forest and saw this brightly coloured bird for the first time, darting between the flowers and only hovering over the red ones. Its wings hummed as it moved swiftly from one flower to the other. They decided to name it a hummingbird because of the pleasant humming sound that it makes with its wings.

That is why the beautiful hummingbird hovers over the mountainside, flying close to the red flowers. One of these colourful birds might be Taroo, who is still searching for his love, Alida.

About the Author

Photo by Matt Shearer

Wendy Shearer is a professional storyteller and writer based in London. She regularly performs stories in schools and institutions across the arts including the British Museum, Shakespeare's Globe, and the Royal Academy of Arts.

Wendy's repertoire of stories is drawn mostly from her Afro-Caribbean ancestry and first degree in Classics. Her background is in writing and producing children's television for CBBC. She is also a member of the Society for Storytelling, actively promoting the ancient art form of oral storytelling. *African and Caribbean Folktales, Myths and Legends* is her first book for children.

Other books in the

SCHOLASTIC CLASSICS collection:

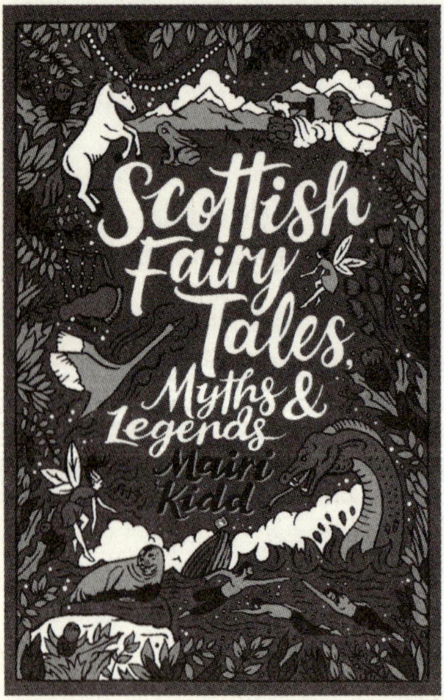